CHARM
CITY
COP

CHARM CITY COP

The Life and Times of Steve Tabeling

John F. Reintzell

iUniverse

CHARM CITY COP
THE LIFE AND TIMES OF STEVE TABELING

iUniverse books may be ordered through booksellers or by contacting:

iUniverse
1663 Liberty Drive
Bloomington, IN 47403
www.iuniverse.com
1-800-Authors (1-800-288-4677)

ISBN: 978-1-5320-5650-5 (sc)
ISBN: 978-1-5320-5651-2 (e)

Library of Congress Control Number: 2018910317

Print information available on the last page.

iUniverse rev. date: 09/26/2018

To my loving wife,
Mary Jane

PREFACE

I have had the privilege of knowing Steve Tabeling for over twenty years, and though I deeply regret that I never had the opportunity to work with or for the man, I knew of him and his stellar reputation nonetheless. I first saw him as he taught a class on stress management while a lieutenant in the police academy, and I was taken by the fact that this man of near celebrity status was a down-to-earth, soft-spoken man of deep convictions: about integrity and ethics and, above all, about the importance of family. He told us that day that each of us should be true to our convictions and beliefs, our sense of duty and integrity, and our loved ones. Being true to those things, he said, would ensure that we would be competent professionals and honorable men and women.

By the time we were both retired, our professional paths crossed again, and I was fortunate to do consultant work with him and then to engage him in the creation and production of quality training designed to equip homicide investigators with the skills and insights that would enable their success. We went on to produce other training seminars together that were delivered to various police and sheriff's departments in Maryland and Virginia.

The opportunity to write Steve's biography was one I could not pass up. My sincerest hope is that I have done justice to the man and his extraordinary careers as I wrote of the incidents and occurrences of his life, as Steve related them to me. Though I have met and worked with and trained literally thousands of law enforcement professionals during my nearly fifty years' involvement in the profession, I can honestly state that I have *never* met a man of Steve Tabeling's exceptional character, wide-ranging capabilities, and pure genuineness. I hope every reader of this book finds him as I have: a tonic for the mediocre, a miracle cure for sorry attitude, and a sterling example of excellence.

John F. Reintzell
Baltimore, Maryland
Winter 2017-18

FOREWORD

While both police officers and prosecutors have essential roles in our criminal justice system, their roles are almost always complimentary rather than collaborative, with the officers responsible for the investigation of criminal activity and the prosecutors responsible for the litigation of criminal charges that result from the investigation. There are, however, exceptions to that general rule. One of those exceptions was the Baltimore Narcotics Strike Force, to which I was assigned while serving as an Assistant State's Attorney for Baltimore City. Funded by an LEAA grant, the Strike Force was staffed by prosecutors working side by side with police officers led by Steve Tabeling.

Getting to know Steve, and the officers he commanded, was the highlight of my assignment to the Strike Force. I served in the State's Attorney's Office for a period of six years, and during that period of time I had the extreme good fortune to work with outstanding police officers and to witness their numerous acts of bravery and personal sacrifice. No officer that I had the privilege of working with was more outstanding than Steve Tabeling, to whom I say, *"Thanks, yet again, for inspiring us by sharing your remarkable experiences!"*

With admiration and respect, Joe Murphy

S teve was the finest law enforcement officer I ever knew or had the opportunity to work with. Our experience together goes back almost 60 years and our law enforcement careers have largely paralleled each other. I was a brand new Assistant State's Attorney just learning the trade when Steve made sergeant. Among the highlights of my young legal career was the prosecution of a burglary or a robbery or a lottery violation investigated by Sergeant Tabeling of the Eastern District. Steve was an indefatigable investigator, an articulate and persuasive witness, and scrupulously honest. I learned at the very outset that he was a man you could totally rely upon.

As I went on to be the Deputy State's Attorney and then the State's Attorney for Baltimore City, the working relationship with then Lieutenant Tabeling became even stronger, as I relied on Steve to spearhead sensitive confidential investigations. His performance was always outstanding.

As I moved on to become a judge of the Court of Special Appeals, I thought my contact with Steve might cease, but that was not to be the case. After his sterling service as the Chief of the Homicide Squad, Steve ultimately took over as Chief of the Police Training Academy and he and I were back in business. A favorite specialty of mine was the Constitutional law of Search and Seizure, and no one was a more avid reader of my opinions than Steve Tabeling, as he then proceeded to teach the intricacies of search and seizure law to the ranks coming through the Police Academy. He was no lawyer, but no lawyer understood the nuances of the *Carroll* Doctrine on automobile searches nearly as thoroughly as did Steve Tabeling.

With a sense of personal pride and satisfaction, I have followed Steve's later career as Chief of Police of Salisbury, Maryland; as Chief of Security of the Johns Hopkins Hospital and Medical School; and as Chief of Security of Loyola College. None of these accomplishments, however, has ever surprised me, for they were just what I would have expected 60 years ago when I first worked with a young Sergeant Tabeling of the Eastern District.

Charles E. Moylan, Jr.
Senior Judge
Maryland Court of Special Appeals

INTRODUCTION

T he city embracing the shoreline of the Patapsco River in
Maryland has played a crucial role in the history and economic
development of the American republic and still occupies an
enviable geographic and topographic location. It is a major world
port, a principal railroad transportation network close to the nation's
capital, and a home to top-tier professional sports teams. It is home
as well to over six hundred thousand people and to world-class
institutions of higher education, medicine, and medical research.
It has been described as a totally charming and unique small town,
once proudly boasting a very high proportion of home ownership.
It is actually many small towns and communities enfolded within a
larger political entity and self-governing city. It is, as it once was, a
good place in which to grow up, a good place to visit and enjoy, and
a good place in which to grow old.

Or maybe not. Once home to nearly a million people, Baltimore,
in the past half century, has seen its image and economic viability
erode steadily, despite impressive, expensive, but ultimately futile
downtown redevelopment efforts, ongoing urban renewal, and
attempts at self-reinvention. The decades from the 1950s to the
present day witnessed wholesale flight of hundreds of thousands of

Baltimore's working and middle-class residents. It was triggered by imprudent governmental programs and schemes conceived with good intentions but that inadvertently contributed to the destabilization of neighborhoods. These epic miscalculations, together with other unmitigated and costly public project failures, depleted the tax base of the city and contributed to the depressingly inevitable decline of the city's once first-rate public school system.

Over everything looms the specter of violence. The only constant through all these years of turmoil is Baltimore's depressingly high rate of violent crime. To an unfortunate extent, the city has devolved into a poster town of horrific images and anecdotes of violence, some distorted and contrived but too many constituting *accurate* images. Four decades ago, Baltimore consistently suffered more than three hundred murders a year, and its most recent crime projections once again approach and surpass those levels of violence in a city with a much-reduced population. There are the complaints of residents that the Baltimore Police Department's top leadership remains aloof, unresponsive, and unproductive. A sizeable list of past commissioners and their relatively short tenures comprise yet another complaint, both from residents and the rank and file of the police department. Frequent changes of chief executives contribute to uncertainty; new leaders appointed invariably emphasize alternative styles of crime fighting and service delivery and further muddle the role and responsibilities of the cop in the patrol car. Stability in top leadership has been lacking for years, often the result of politicians grown tired of excuses as to why violent crime cannot be curtailed.

Plummeting morale among cops produces huge gaps in actual versus authorized strength levels—hundreds of *vacant positions* at a time when the recruitment of new law enforcement officers is a very challenging mission.

The men and women who have prevented Baltimore from complete meltdown during the past half century are the city's police and fire department members, blue collar employees who have consistently put the city's welfare ahead of their own and who have never failed to intervene to restore order when order was at risk and when competently led, often at hazard to their own safety, indeed survival. Such dedication, professionalism, and competence are commonplace and hardly remarkable to the thousands of citizens who live and work in the city.

A converse segment of the public service spectrum is personified by many elected and appointed officials who comprise city government. To be sure, the varied and vital services essential to the function of a complex urban area could not happen without them. But there are, as well, officials who have wandered into the sea of tranquility, flowing *with* events rather than influencing them; and those officials who benefit from their roles within government.

They oversee the maintenance and operation of the police and fire departments, public works, transportation, waste management, recreation and parks, community centers, schools, facility maintenance, finance, and the myriad essential functions without which the quality of life would be immeasurably degraded. Alas, the infrastructure essential to a city rests upon an archaic and decaying waste and sewer system that malfunctions, bursts, or otherwise fails with alarming regularity and a transportation network hardly worthy of the name. To the credit of the architects and engineers who built it, the water system still transmits water of sterling quality, a testament to the vision, industry, and foresight of those nineteenth-century designers who built it and to those of current years who struggle to repair and maintain it. But infrastructure cannot continue to function adequately in the face of expedient repairs that constitute quick fixes. No money is available to comprehensively overhaul the entire system. For many of the elevated roadways, sewers, water delivery, and bridge systems, time is simply running out.

Then there is a school system that has lost half of its students in the past twenty years, in large measure because it fails to teach children to adequately read, write, or think; *and* because of the violence endemic in many schools, violence that reflects the reality of each school's surrounding neighborhoods—depressingly the same through the decades. A school administration that appears incapable of controlling the most ordinary of events within its purview—ensuring heated school buildings on cold days, for example—and which seems to be a magnet for money lavished upon it, largely by the state government, to a point that the Baltimore Department of Education spends more than fifteen thousand dollars per capita on its students, nearly tops in the nation and produces a dismal outcome: children who complete the grades and still cannot read or write. Unemployable graduates.

Though Baltimore is not unlike other elderly East Coast urban areas, all of which suffer from aging infrastructure, in Baltimore there appears to be no comprehensive long-term plan in place to systematically address such critical issues. Rather, there have been politically motivated stratagems intended to erect public structures, or merely hugely expensive projects at public expense so as to get one's political persona indelibly inscribed on public consciousness now and in the years to come: a $300 million downtown hotel that hemorrhages tens of millions of dollars from the city's annual operating budget; a second convention center also costing nearly $300 million and chronically underutilized; a red line rail system ticketed at a hefty $3 billion and mercifully nixed by Maryland's popular governor, Larry Hogan.

Finally, the current plans at urban *improvement* involve razing whole blocks of masonry residences that once were the envy of other cities because they were well-built brick structures, affordable, and thus often owned by working-class men and women. The improvement accrued? More vacant lots.

Unique as a place, Baltimore possesses a nineteenth-century uniqueness in its governance as well. In Tabeling's day, the reigning police commissioner, Donald D. Pomerleau, a former US Marine Corps field grade officer, was appointed by the governor of Maryland, a huge factor in allowing him to bypass corrupt and sometimes brutal local politics. Chief executives of the Baltimore Police Department could thumb their noses at the mayor and City Council—up to a point; the local politicos still controlled the purse strings. But practically speaking, the day-to-day operations of the police department were pretty much left up to the reigning commissioner.

This gave them powers usually reserved for elected officials, a point not lost on a succession of Baltimore's mayors.

Just as the monarchy defined the English nation state and its succeeding generations, Donald D. Pomerleau became the definitive commissioner of the Baltimore Police Department. To the chagrin of a succession of Baltimore mayors, Donald Pomerleau wielded his considerable powers untrammeled by the vagaries of local politics, a freedom to reign that was unprecedented in his time and envied by subsequent executives.

Pomerleau had risen through the ranks of the Marine Corps, and he had definitive ideas about leadership, organizational decorum, and discipline. He was not a man to suffer fools at all, and the underling called into the commissioner's presence knew in short order exactly where he stood in the realm.

To be sure, Pomerleau dragged the Baltimore Police organization and its members into its heyday—enforcing higher standards of crime reporting, discipline, performance, and behavior, both on and off the job. Fair-haired scions were defined by their abilities and intellects; the Department in the sixties identified the importance of advanced education, rigorous professional inspections, and the military's penchant for holding people accountable. Disdaining specialization, the reigning commissioner declared every cop to be a generalist. He emphasized the vital nature of establishing and maintaining good relations with the town's numerous neighborhoods and community associations; ostensibly he decentralized authority, maintaining clout for his district and on-scene commanders, while quietly maintaining ultimate dominion from his headquarters building. If he committed one miscue it involved taking officers off their foot posts and putting them in cars, the better to get there faster. The business community took it hard.

To be a cop in any American city demands brains, courage, and an eye on the goal line, while quick-stepping to the minuet of political correctitude. But Steve Tabeling was never much of a dancer. He was ill equipped, either culturally or mentally, to blend in with the background noise, adhere to wrong-headed tactics, or waste time on worn clichés. He viewed all such as wasteful of time and downright dumb. Simply put, Tabeling got to the point in the most direct manner he could. The rule was *don't do wrong*. That meant *consistent with the rule of law.*

PROLOGUE

T he substitute teacher stood comfortably before his public school class. As he waited for quiet, he considered the faces of each child. They were mostly white kids with a few Hispanics and some black children, and their voices revealed their collective curiosity and apprehension. They waited impatiently to see what this old man was about.

To Tabeling they looked like pretty good kids. He stood before them, quietly and square-shouldered, and talked slowly and with confidence.

"My name is Mr. Tabeling," he said. "Your teacher is not here, because she is under the weather today, and I am going to try to take her place." The children buzzed and rolled their eyes or lolled in their seats. Tabeling was grateful to be assigned to a second-grade class; seven-year-olds seemed so much more reasonable than the junior-high-schoolers he had experienced in his new career as a substitute. In fact, he thought some of them were on their way to prison, with high school as just a pit stop before their inevitable end point.

"We're going to start with your reading lessons from yesterday. First, who didn't do their homework?" The children let out a collective giggle, but only one was brave enough to raise her hand. Tabeling elevated his eyebrows at her. "Why not?" he asked.

"My parents didn't pick me up until late from my grandmother's last night, and I … um … fell asleep on the way home." The class, especially the girls, twittered at this.

"Well," Tabeling said, "we'll let it go this time. Open your reading books to page nineteen. Who wants to start?"

Several hands went up, and he selected the most enthused.

The reading class was as much an exercise in memorizing the *look* of words as it was of sounding them out or of grasping some sliver of phonics.

His thoughts vectored back to many years past when he had been a little boy and had occupied a desk in a classroom. He thought back to how very much he had hated school. It had been a burning, visceral aversion to the limits on his freedom that the schoolroom had inflicted. Over eighty years later, his application as a substitute teacher listed several advanced degrees from a prestigious university—and over forty years as a cop, a campus security director, and a police chief. What had happened between his second-grade experience and who he was today was a journey nearly too exceptional to recount.

He listened patiently as the child began her reading.

"When the brown cow was let out of the barn, it didn't know whether to go up or down the pasture. Up the hill was sweet grass and clover, but it had been chewed to bare spots. Down the hill was thick with dark green grass but was very wet. It was hard for the cow to pull any up."

"Good." Mr. Tabeling stopped her. "Who's next?"

CHAPTER

1

Steve Tabeling was a product of the same streets he later policed, and he was the image of the street smarts that one day would make him an outstanding investigator—and a very well-educated one. His learning, however, did not come easy.

As a boy he absorbed several critical shocks at a vulnerable age. Shock number one: Without his consent or knowledge, his parents forcibly moved him from a shore home on the scenic Magothy River—a boy's paradise—to the city of Baltimore on Wilcox Street, a side street with views of nothing other than similar drably appointed brick homes. That was a cruel adjustment for the six-year-old. That had been quite bad enough, but what followed was apocalyptic. Shock two happened without warning when one morning he was dragged by his father to Saint James Catholic Elementary School. Even worse than the first unwelcome change, the school entry trauma was a disaster.

Yanked there by his dad, Stephen Tabeling Jr., the unwilling new student broke free and climbed the steps of the church, which sat adjacent to the classroom building, and threw his books in a looping arc into the street. His dad, quite enraged, carried him off the steps and compelled him to enter and take a seat in the classroom. As soon as his father departed to go to work, little Steve excited the ire of the tiny teaching nun. Adopting a passive aggression that would do credit to an adult, young Tabeling studiously ignored everything being instructed the entire first day, before the day ended, she broke a bamboo cane across the boy's back. Little Steve adamantly refused to return the next day until his father, squeezed for time by his work and in desperation, enlisted the aid of the local cop, Officer Bill Lutz, who was to accompany little Steve to school on a daily basis. Their paths would cross years later.

Dodges to sidestep school abounded. With patience and curiosity, little Steve discovered two helpful tidbits: (1) the nuns discouraged the attendance of any of their little students who suffered from diarrhea, and (2) ingestion of a single Carter's Little Liver Pill, bisected, induced the loose bowel condition that provided blessed freedom from that day's classes. When that tactic paled, there was always a safe harbor at his paternal grandparents' home, Elvie and Steve Tabeling. Still another safe harbor, was the welcoming home of his maternal grandmother, Catherine Noonan, an Irish girl from County Cork, whose lilting brogue beguiled the young boy so that he kept her place dear in his heart. Far better than listening to the nun drone about religion and arithmetic, Grandmom regaled him with fantastic stories about leprechauns and their special powers—exaggerations, they were, and even as a child Steve saw through her fabrications, though charmingly told.

And there was Grandfather Steve, the towering, strong, and calm giant of a man who did not criticize, scold, or make him go to school. The grandparents peopled the island that was his refuge.

A day on the town for a little boy in 1935 Baltimore was an adventure unparalleled. Freedom—the noisy, dirty city became his paradise to be explored and savored.

Life for the average person was quite bleak. The Depression had hammered the mercantile and economic pulse of all of America's cities and its countryside, like a silent storm that carried all before it. Even before its full force had been felt several years before, one in five workers were without work; one family in six was forced to accept relief, a hand-out. Soup kitchens were besieged by hungry men and women, and many went to bed accompanied only by the rustling sounds in their bellies. Children were hardly exempt from this hardship. Little Steve recalled many days of going to school (on the days when his school dodging devices sputtered) without breakfast and no lunch and returning to home to cabbage, string beans, and smoked neck—filling and cheap foods to satisfy the four children in the Tabeling household by then. Times were desperate, not even a penny each to buy penny candy.

Steve Jr. was fortunate to find work wherever work could be found: auto mechanic, pipe fitter, construction, anything mechanical. His knowledge and talent put food on the table, if not always steadily. A talented musician, he also was a gifted baseball player as a catcher and had been scouted by professional teams, but he viewed playing the sport for money as objectionable. Steve, as father, was demanding of his children; he was hardworking when he could find work and good-hearted. He had a fourth-grade education, but he was gifted in mathematics, able to calculate complex formulas for fitting and cutting components at a job site.

When he was sober.

At other times, the demon alcohol took as deathly a grip of him as is possible for a dependence to take. More often than not, he made no appearance at home following a workday, instead hollowing an indentation into the bar called Gayhart's Tavern at Oliver and Chester Streets. Little Steve was savvy enough at age six to knock on the side door of the tavern and ask for his father. When he came to the door, the boy asked for any spare change his father might be holding and was never refused.

Steve's mother was also Catherine, like her mother, though she was not patient with her ungovernable firstborn son, who steadfastly supported the cause of truancy, coupled with his tendency to run the streets and generally avoid much about home, other than sleeping there. "You're a schemer," she scolded him. Catherine birthed six babies on a severely tight budget and was a patient and strong woman who awaited her prodigal husband's return, usually in the early morning each day. Patience was not her strongest trait.

Not all was bleak. During times when Steve Jr. could maintain his work focus, he was talented enough to form his own business venture, work unknown to modern times, by contracting to convert home coal-burning furnaces to oil burners. He had spotty success but not because his work was flawed; rather, it was because of his alcohol addiction and his inability to accept advice from anyone. During the flush years, however, food became more plentiful in the household. He could even afford a truck for use in the business.

By age fourteen, young Steve was assisting his dad with the work, learning electrical and mechanical trade skills, though he stood only four foot nine and weighed ninety-five pounds.

But all that was in the future.

For his largely unpleasant 1935 present, young Steve made a dubious living when not otherwise forced to attend classes at Saint James, trolling for discarded bottles, which, in that cash-poor time, were worth a nickel a piece—big change to almost anyone but a really big deal to a six-year-old. A week's effort could net enough for an occasional movie admission, just enough to get off the street for a bit; slow to a pause.

The boy's rebelliousness had a basis. Poverty was a big part of it. Sleep and food deprivation ranked high as well. But inside the six-year-old there was more going on than even educated professionals of the day could have deduced. He suffered from acute anxiety—a mind-numbing panic that clouded the sunniest day and pressed him deep into himself. It showed itself in varied ways, the most severe of which triggered a petrifying terror and fear of being abandoned. Undiagnosed, the condition festered and worsened as the boy aged. It produced *de-realization*—an eerie out-of-body experience. *What is happening to me*? he thought constantly. Nothing that was real made any sense to him, and that terrified him further.

Eventually, slowly and painfully, the first-grader began to adjust and attend his classes. He even began to adapt to the strict Catholic classroom and to the regulated routines, even to the discipline the nuns administered. He saw that there were useful things in the school—paper and pencils; things he might learn to use. Little by little, the boy began to gather the import of reading and writing. Though chronically distracted, he began to take in at least a bit of what the nun shared with her class.

Insecurity was reignited in the boy when the family was forced to relocate, dictated by the reality that father Steve could not stay sober long enough to hold down steady work. The move was the first of several to find cheaper rooms for the growing family. With each new neighborhood came new schools. The boy was taken from Saint James and enrolled in Saint Dominic's, then placed in Saint Paul's, and then back to Saint Dominic's. Each time his frustration and fears worsened. In hindsight, the moves comprised a near-classic experiment that prompted in the child progressively worse insolence and more aggressive behavior, which was certain to provoke a stern and sometimes physical attitude adjustment from the no-nonsense sisters, and which inflamed progressively worse attitude and even worse behavior in him.

As the years and the schools came and went, with each new classroom the boy dug deeper into himself, withdrawing to the safe core that sheltered and sustained him. Most days he dressed and was out the door without breakfast, books, lunch, or desire. His truancies mounted, and by the third and fourth grades, it was an odd day when he attended. This was in an era when communications between teachers and parents was parlous at best, and the child was able to absent himself on nearly a full-time basis—report cards that listed his absences usually failed to make it home.

When there was time, he used a pencil to practice the cursive writing the nun tried to teach him. At first looking at other handwriting he found in his house, he tried hard to produce something that looked similar. And then he noticed that once his scribble began to develop, his scrawls looked much like the writing his mother did when she left a note for the milkman or a note for his father, returning home yet again beyond midnight. With some practice and a peek at her signings on the various letters, grocery ledgers, and the like, the boy was able to produce a pretty good likeness of his mother's signature. From then on, there were no more "lost" report cards; no more annoyed nuns demanding the return of the parental signed card. In that little bit of effort and creativity, little Steve fathomed that there was a connection between learning and freedom from worry.

After all, it was his granddad, his Pop, who shelled out the thirty-five cents a week tuition, entrusting it to Steve's small hand each Monday. And his Pop, the boy reasoned—a gentle, easygoing giant of a man—would not mind if he took the day off to make some change by finding (sometimes *filching*) stray pop bottles from wherever. Pop was a hardworking man who knew about making money, and the boy knew his Pop would understand that a hustling, hardworking grandson needed something to throw down his throat—a cream soda, maybe, the kind that was delicious and cost thirty-five cents. It was not worth a second thought—not until one day when, after a hard afternoon of finding and redeeming bottles by the score, the boy was resting in the front parlor of their current home. It was a day all the more remarkable because both his mother and his father were also home together.

Staring absently through the large window from his stuffed chair, the boy was riveted by a sight he had never before witnessed. Approaching with resolute step, somewhat hunched forward as he progressed, was his Pop. His body moved with a purposeful momentum, as though weighed down by something important. In that sickening moment, young Steve divined what it was, and without a thought, he hurled his body through the back bedroom, out of the house, and across the back street and deep into the adjoining woods. There, he crouched beneath a wild bush. Breathing audibly, he tried to make his heart stop pounding so loudly that he was sure it could be heard across the street.

"Stephen!" he heard his father shouting. "Where *are* you?" His voice a bit shriller than the boy had ever before heard it, a fact that did not calm him in the least. Before another minute passed, the boy heard the crashing of men through the underbrush and around the trees nearby. He thought his heart was going to explode.

"Stephen!" the man bellowed again, only this time the sound seemed near enough to touch.

"There he is. Grab him!" his normally placid Pop shouted.

He was caught and heaved from his hiding place by his father. Both men were grim-faced and said not a word as they hauled him across the street and back into the house. What ensued was calculated to badly torpedo the boy's serenity—and it was life-altering.

Pop remained the calm presence. After he told his enraged son to "leave the boy alone." the older man sat Steve beside him and took a minute for the boy, shaking with fright, to get calm as well. "Stephen," he said quietly. "You have to realize that you have a good brain. And you must learn to use it for something good."

As discipline, it was a balm to the boy's frenzied nerves. He was not going to get punished—not by anything physical—and that was a welcome and totally unexpected development. Though he saw that his father was not taking any of this well, the old man's presence and strength was sufficient to forestall any physical unpleasantness.

Sometimes when he was caught knee-deep in some dereliction, the boy could expect a severe and swift reaction. Other times, even when he hadn't done something bad, severity erupted unexpectedly, originating from his father's frustrations either with his oldest boy's distracted mode of living, or the boy's apathy, or his inability to see through to the cause-and-effect of his actions. Too often his father waited to admonish him at the dinner table, in front of the whole family.

"You," his father often told him, while pressing his thumb against the last joint of his little finger, "have about this much sense compared to your brother."

In retrospect, the boy's life had been a cycle with a predictable outcome. By age nine, Steve's father was called to Saint Dominic's and brusquely informed that his child was no longer welcome in the school.

Expulsion had never entered the family's plans for their oldest child. A public school was the only remaining alternative, and the boy was enrolled in Broadway Junior High. If Steve Jr. expected the boy's dismissal from Catholic school to have infused some penitence or behavior modification in his son, he was shortly disabused of the notion. As though the nuns had played an unintentional role in little Steve's blossoming delinquency, the boy now was more than ever determined to be done with this business of classrooms, boring subjects, and insipid teachers. He threw his efforts into skipping school on a full-time basis. The days were his once again, and he could scarcely conceal his relief at the prospect.

As his trespasses flourished, the boy sought more forays into impulsiveness. His Pop drove a glistening black Chevrolet, and each workday he parked the car at his place of work and then left the keys in his locker. Although absent a driver's license, little Steve considered how grand it would be to drive such a car, and so he slipped into the locker room of the company, found his Pop's locker, and was instantly transported to new driver status, tooling the large vehicle eastward to the Herring Run Park, with a friend as his front-seat passenger. The trip, especially the driving part, was a highlight, and driving the borrowed machine became his passion. "I don't know what's wrong with that machine," Pop would say, "but it's burning a lot of gas lately."

As if such wrongdoing was not enough to provoke the fates, if Pop's car keys could not be gotten for whatever reason, Dad's had to do. Dad's was not a prestige vehicle—actually, it was a battered former hearse and looked to the boy to be a block long. Never mind, he reasoned; he could haul more of his friends around the places in town that he knew and explore those he did not yet know.

After motoring to an interesting part of town and parking the ponderous vehicle at a curb, he strolled contentedly with his friends. All was peachy until the boy spied a police officer standing on the walk just ahead. Something must have attracted the officer's attention as the boys, returning from a foray on foot, approached "their" car. The officer correctly discerned the ringleader and pointed directly at Steve, asking, "This yours?" He then demanded the boy show his license.

Without a second's hesitation, little Steve produced his *father's* license, which he'd had the forethought to swipe as well—and with the birth date clearly listed as 1905. The officer scanned the license for an eternity. "Okay," he said at last as he returned the document. "Drive safely."

So the days melted into weeks, untrammeled by the fetid schoolhouse and its bad-smelling classrooms. At length, Steve clamored at his mother to quit school so that his truancy record and his fears of discovery would be likewise expunged. She frowned at such a request and refused, time after time. Eventually, though, he wore her down. With his father's reluctant okay, she accompanied him to the principal's office at the junior high, signed parental permission slip in hand.

Presented with the decision that was totally driven by the boy's desire to be free, the principal, a crisp and polite middle-aged man, frowned as though thoroughly perplexed by the request. "Why, Mrs. Tabeling," he told her, "we already have a file record that he withdrew with parental permission. That was *last year,* according to our records." He then proceeded to show the shocked mother the permission slip with her "signature" at its bottom.

None of this endeared the boy to his father. "You don't want to go to school," Steve Jr. told his oldest son, "then you're going to go work. With *me.*"

And so the fourteen-year-old concluded his truncated academic career—he hoped forever—and became a hardworking apprentice in the business his father did: tearing out the insides of coal-burning home furnaces—a dirty, noisome, and arduous labor. Conditions varied for each job, but basements became the boy's province— normally dank, dark and choked with debris, dusty, and occasionally vermin-infested. No matter, the boy reasoned; he was to earn up to twenty dollars a week—a fortune in 1943, especially for an adolescent who lived at home, though the possibility of not being paid by his tavern-hopping father wised up little Steve soon enough. He made it his business to track his dad at week's end and shadow him as well, if that's what it took to get his money. He was, after all, a kid who viewed his future through the prism of one day at a time, not surprising for someone giddy with the prospects the money held for him, though his mother was less than thrilled by the entire venture.

There were complications to working with his father, who rarely concealed his contempt for his oldest boy and for the chaotic manner in which he was living his life. Most days they worked together but separately, as physically removed from each other as they were emotionally distant, and little Steve was grateful for that. While the work engulfed him, it did more; it insulated him from the nameless fears that grew deep within him. The older he got, the more he experienced them. They were the worst at night; often he lay awake, terrified to sleep, afraid that he would never waken. The feeling engulfed and threatened to drown him, and he had no one to whom he could turn. Once, desperate to unburden himself to someone, he turned to his parents, tearfully telling all as they sat, skeptical and grim-faced. With the truth out, he awaited some solace, some measure of reassurance.

"You're *loose-headed*," was his mother's scornful assertion, to which his father nodded agreement. Desperate to have relief from the demons that besieged his daytime terrors, he began each morning to duck into church when he found its massive doors unlocked. There, before daily mass was began, he sat within the gloom of the towering walls and darkened stained glass, asking the Almighty to make this terrible thing leave him alone. Then—and for years to come—he knelt each day in silent prayers that went unanswered.

The rest of each day, the boy's head, as well as his thoughts, was in the furnaces he worked to convert. At least the work was straightforward enough. Once gutted, the old furnace box was retained to house the new oil burner, which efficiently heated water to circulate in the house's radiators. This process distributed clean and safe heated air, emitted via radiant warmth, and ensured comfort, even in the coldest of Baltimore winters. But first the bottom of the iron brute had to be relined with fire-resistant bricks that contained asbestos. Stooping on his knees, the boy carefully built up the inner structure until its interior walls were covered. As he grew adept, his father showed him an additional chore that he could do—wiring the newly installed thermostats, which was exacting but essential work. As he grew confident, he got hired by electricians who assisted Steve Jr., and his confidence and expanded skill set increased. He was a working man—to heck with classrooms!

When not at work, he was learning in his own way. His inquisitive nature searched out and explored whatever crossed his path. The boy knew his father was a musician who played a very respectable trumpet, which he stored in its case at their current home. One day little Steve opened the case and put the mouthpiece to his lips, producing a recognizable musical note on his very first try. His Pop heard the effort and asked the boy if this was something he wanted to try, thinking that any such diversion might go far to straightening out his grandson's erratic and unproductive behavior. He would pay for the boy to have lessons, and little Steve jumped at the opportunity. Finally, there was a formal learning setting on which he didn't want to skip out, and as his knowledge grew, so too did his musical abilities. His Pop marveled; the child had a knack for music and actually seemed to enjoy practicing. Before long, little Steve wondered if he might be good enough to join a school band. Saint Dominic's had just such a band—a marching school band, whose members turned out in very elegant uniforms, tailor-fit garments donated by parishioners and businessmen. Just like that, he belonged to something grand, something that made him proud. It was a first.

Just like that, the boy had a focal point that channeled his restlessness and eased his fears somewhat. Focus was so important to any youth growing up in a large, poor family during hard times. A sense of belonging to something gave joy to many: the band members, their parents and families, and the audiences for whom they played. All of that made sense to him, as though nothing before the music and the band really had resonated. No other aim or purpose had touched him before this. Although the terrors still consumed him most of the day and lots of the nights, the thought of making music in concert with the others became his North Star.

As if that was not enough, another, more momentous thing occurred. Before he'd gotten his first payday from his father, he hit up a friend for a quarter to go to the movies. Climbing the steps into the balcony, he spotted an empty seat and made for it. "That seat is taken," a young girl in the adjacent seat told him.

"I know," he sassed. "Because I just took it." He was about to add a flourish to his brazenness, but his embryonic witticism was interrupted in mid-thought.

"You're in my seat," said a pretty girl who had just returned from the popcorn stand. "You need to sit somewhere else."

"If you want to sit here, you'll have to sit in my lap," the boy responded with a smile. He noticed that she was not only feisty and forceful, but she was pretty, with short dark-blonde hair and dressed neatly.

But her pretty face was contorted by a fierce frown, and she refused to back down. "That'll be the day," she said with a sniff. "You are in my seat, and you need to leave it and me alone. The movie's starting!"

Others in the audience were beginning to take note of the exchange, and more than a few of them frowned at him for the disturbance. The boy didn't care. He liked this particular seat he had found; he liked the view, and it was his, plain and simple. Still, the movie was starting, and he couldn't sit there with this girl at his knee, nor could he ignore that angry stare she directed his way. Finally, he relented and, with a smile, removed himself from the girl's seat—but only as far as a vacant seat across the aisle. He liked that view as well, and he contorted his slender form ninety degrees to his left so that the girl—not the blaring, shimmering movie screen—became his entire focal point. To the extent that she noticed him at all, it was to more studiously ignore the rude boy; perhaps she was relieved that he had removed himself.

He sat with craned neck for the entire film and only realized it had ended when people got up to leave. Not willing to be left in her wake as she rose to exit with her girlfriend, he made up his mind to follow her home. On the way there, she turned once, abruptly, to fix him with her angry glare. "You better stop following me," she warned him. He took not the least notice and continued after her. Something—he didn't know what—propelled him.

At long last she reached her house in the 700 block of East Preston Street, climbed the steps gingerly, and entered. He could not follow but stood for a moment to drink it in. Then he turned on his heel and headed for home.

Chance meeting it had been. Funny thing, though—he couldn't get her off his mind. She was pretty, true enough. But there was much more to her than that. The way she spoke up for herself. Like what was hers, *was hers*, which included her privacy. She wasn't shy, and in an adolescent conception of that, he knew that she was like him, someone not above poking anyone in the jaw who got in his space.

Maybe there was more to it, because he was a person inclined to be *to himself.* He preferred that. And his fright probably made him like that. When he was never certain that what he saw or heard was really real, it became a wall between him and the world, most especially people. When he ran the streets, he was his own person, and he knew that he could depend on himself. The people around him might be friends, impediments, adversaries, or phantoms. Some helped him; others—like most teachers—got in the way. What mattered was that he kept himself moving forward, succeeding no matter what.

But succeeding at what? He was still a kid, but already he was totally in the routine of working. And it *was* work, for certain. But in the dimly lit basements of the neighborhoods where his father got jobs, the boy could connect and focus on the furnace before him. The work, not just the money it brought, brought him a kind of peace; a freedom from the feeling that he had to run. Like the music. Things—new, interesting things—hit him fast. He was all of fourteen, and he was on a course.

But to where? he wondered.

When he took the time to think about it, his home life, the work, and the band all were pretty good things, but instinctively he felt that they were not enough. He felt he was lacking something. There needed to be more, something much more. His mind wandered as he placed each brick along the interior of the ash-bin holder beneath the dismantled furnace. *If this is the way that life is supposed to be,* he thought, *there really is not a lot to recommend it.*

Though he was glad enough to earn some money so he had food to get him through the day, even as a youth he imagined a life just of that and nothing more. *There has to be more,* he thought. Something of value, like the music he made. Something that *meant* something.

Stephen and Catherine (Noonan)
Tabeling, Jr. - Steve's parents

Stephen and Elvie Tabeling,
Sr. - Steve's Grandparents

Josephine (Skipper) and Jacob Bailey -
Steve's Great Grandparents

Steve III, Elvie, Beverly and Bob
(Nora not pictured) Siblings

Steve III and Bob

Steve's brother, Billy

CHAPTER

The next day he again recollected the look of the girl in the movie house. He remembered that, like him, she was short—four foot eleven or so. If she had stood motionless for a minute, they might have stared into each other's eyes. Now she seemed lost to him. It was ridiculous.

But he brightened as the thought came to him: He knew where she lived. It was summer. Maybe she sat out on the front step each night, like everybody in his neighborhood did. Without another second's thought, he resolved a plan. And at the end of his workday, he left his job behind him and headed up Broadway to seek her out.

As he neared the neighborhood, he glimpsed the tall, stately, three-story brick homes that lined the street, each with a concrete stoop leading up to its entrance. Her house was near the end of the 700 block of Preston. As he approached, he saw immediately that he'd been right. People were perched, several on each set of steps, chatting amiably. He spotted her address, and there beneath the house numbers was the girl, sitting among her companions—a girl and two boys. Without hesitation, he approached.

"There's that boy that followed me home," he heard her say, loudly enough for him—and the neighbors—to overhear.

"Do you remember me from the movies?" he asked, oblivious to her very apparent displeasure at seeing him. "I came here to see you again. I want to ask you out."

"Yes," she responded, "I do remember you. And no, I am not going out with you. Now go away. Leave me alone. And stop bothering me."

Not in the least deterred by her rejection, he kept at it. "Okay," he said evenly. "But I'm going to keep coming here to see you until you change your mind."

And in the weeks that followed, he was better than his word. Every night he returned to approach her on her perch. No refusal, brush-off, snub, or strident demand for him to leave discouraged him one speck. He had seen her and liked her, and he was going out with her and that was that. Possibly this was because she was the first person—the first *girl* person—that he'd ever seen (they had not even met, not properly) who even remotely interested him. Maybe it was her fiery expression when she was mad, or her dark blonde hair, or her forceful behavior. Anyway, it was something—the way she carried herself, as though nothing or no one in the whole world was going to tell her to do something she didn't want to do. No one.

What she didn't seem to notice at that moment was that this annoying, skinny boy was just as stubborn as she was.

Like lightning in the sky, his summer sped by. There was work, trekking to the girl's house (again rejected or, worse, merely snubbed), then home, sleep, and the promise of the same thing the next day. But four nights a week he hurried to band practice at Saint James. On those days, the bottomless lake of his energy served him well.

To be a member of a marching band was a privilege, one that had to be earned. There was the music, quite an education in its own right, and then the formation marching. Together, it occupied fully both his thoughts and his movements. But even more important was the conduct that was demanded and the maturity it conveyed. It was expected behavior that went with membership—the simple act of committing, showing up faithfully and on time, ready to practice. And it was being part of something—a grand tradition—that set the musicians apart from others their age. They were fourteen to seventeen years old.

A war was being fought across the globe, and many of the members had older brothers, uncles, or even fathers in the armed forces and at risk. Although they still were children, all thirty-nine members of the band knew that they were representing more than themselves. The Catholic Drum and Bugle Corps included twenty-seven marching bands; each represented a school in the Baltimore Archdiocese. It was part of an old and honored institution and was a very serious deal. It *mattered*, and young Steve felt, for the first time, a tug toward belonging to something bigger than himself.

The marching was never easily done. The entire corps had to move as one. There were no commands given. The maneuvers—forward, left march, rear march, halt, about face—all were accomplished in unison and in sync with predetermined bars in the musical score. The members marched to the sounds of the stirring melody as they played it. It was genuinely orchestrated: form, function, sound, and movement.

Even though he no longer attended school, he could be with the band, play music, and compete. It was the first thing in his life thus far that made him feel as though he could be normal, that he counted for something—something fine. The music was challenging, but the brass trumpets and big bass drums were musical sounds made for each other, as though there had never been such stunningly American music played or heard anywhere before. And though on first hearing the music, the resonances evoked images of the military, the melodic union of brass and percussion lent itself to any melody—show tunes, marches, even the occasional aria.

Best of all, he realized that the harmony and melodic fusion of notes calmed him. For the first time in as long as he could recall, he didn't feel like something was drowning him in choking gray clouds and confusion and terror. The music soothed his soul and made him feel safe and connected to others—an island of calm in the channel of his emotions.

Three or four evenings each week, the boys gathered to practice, first in the schoolyard at Saint James, where they formed their ranks and marched in unison. Later in the summer, as the date of the annual competition drew nearer, they convened at Clifton Park. Unlike the brick-and-mortar confines of the schoolyard, the park provided ample space that made more complex maneuvers possible. It also accustomed the boys to wide spaces, ideal conditioning for the annual Labor Day competition on the playing field at Memorial Stadium, the towering, cavernous sports venue and perfect site to showcase the musical competition that annually attracted upward of forty thousand ardent spectators. The thought of performing there was enough of a spur to gain and hold adolescent imaginations. When he played and marched, his world focused into sharp detail, and it was good.

Still, when not in band practice, he couldn't forget the girl he had seen and talked to. Despite her vocal protests against his presence in her world, her looks of dismissal and firm refusal to have anything to do with him attracted rather than repelled young Steve. Maybe it was the contrariness in him. He thought of her thick blonde hair and determined expression, and he smiled. And he resolved that he would not stop his new practice of stopping by her house each night, even if it meant yet another rejection, because he felt a confidence he didn't even know he possessed. She was not yet an obsession to him. Not yet. But she was getting to him. And he knew that he would wear her down.

She was Dolores Margaret Varley. Like him, she was fourteen, a curious blend of reticent and vibrant teenager. She was a very bright student and had won a partial tuition assistance award on her academic skills, which made it possible for her to attend Seton, one of the city's elite private schools, a Catholic girls-only high school in downtown Baltimore. Her life reflected old values—she was fully attuned to the value of an education and the value of a few trusted friends and family; no more than that. Her parents were divorced, and she lived in the Preston Street house with her sister, her brother, and their mother, Virginia. Within her sheltered world, the girl felt safe and loved. There was no room for anyone from outside her circle.

At his home, the boy's life deteriorated. There were no fights as such, just curt and cutting comments from both his mother and father. In later years, the boy would reason that perhaps his father was seeing his oldest son in the glare of his own failures—failure to hold down steady work, or to come home for supper, or to be a father to his children, or to stop his drinking. Maybe the older man thought he foresaw a dismal future for an undereducated boy, for whom no amount of persuasion seemed sufficient to cure him of his reckless disregard for rules, conventions, and order. Perhaps the father foresaw another future house full of ill-nourished children and a wife darkly censorious of her husband and his flaws.

"I brought you into this world," his father muttered menacingly one day. "And I can take you out of it."

It was the opposite of a nurturing home, and he felt the depth of their disdain as each year passed. The mere act of his growing up seemed to trigger more resentment from them. He spent as little time there as he could. He needed to find work and get out on his own. But at just fourteen years old, he weighed just ninety-five pounds and looked sickly—no one was lining up to offer him work. Then he hit on a plan. He procured a baptismal certificate from the parish office and then got ink eradicator and changed his birth year from 1929 to 1927. That made him sixteen and a much better applicant for a good-paying job. Then began his tireless trek in search of employment.

Before his sixteenth birthday truly arrived, he got a job at the Acme Grocery store, stocking produce. It paid well, and it got him away from his father for a time. When they let him go, he went to work for Washington Federal. When he was let go once again, he got a position as a Western Union delivery boy, walking his deliveries downtown or hopping street cars when necessary. He got to know the streets and neighborhoods that way. Then he worked in a printing establishment, learning the fundamentals of that trade. Intermittently, he returned to work with his father again. The money was good—as long as he caught up to his dad on Fridays when pay was due. Failure to do that meant that no pay would be forthcoming and that he had forfeited a week's work. It was yet another life lesson, painful but practical.

He learned other things as well. His father taught him how to wire the electrical components in the furnace, the thermostat and switches. Electricians working with his dad taught him as well, and young Steve was sharp enough to gain and store each new skill that came his way. He never knew when the skill would pay off, so a little at a time, he learned the value of learning.

Then there were moments when his father displayed a softer parental side, occasionally telling the boy to play his trumpet for a neighbor. When he did, his father seemed to glow with an emotion that looked like quiet pride in his oldest son. It was good for the boy, but it was perplexing as well.

One day, for what reason he knew not (even many years later), the girl consented to let him approach and talk to her. Then he hardly knew where to begin. He opened his bid by asking her out yet again, expecting another refusal. When she said, "I guess so," that was all he needed to hear. He was beside himself with elation. They would go to the movies. Then bowling. It was one of those events that was long anticipated, yet a night when the hours flew by. It was all he could do to fill the time between bowling frames with something witty to say, something interesting at least.

As the end of their evening together hurtled toward him, she turned his way and said with some finality, "This is probably the first and last time."

Despite her somber prediction, in time he got to know that she was Dolores and that she lived with her mother, brother, and sister. And that she was smart as well as pretty. Book smart. School smart. And that her family and friends didn't call her Dolores; they called her *Honey.* As he got to know her better, he began to see and sense her sweetness. Once her estimation of him began to moderate, she listened to his stories, listened as he talked about his music and his hopes. A precocious girl, she had sensed something was amiss in this strange, shy, nervous boy almost from the first, but she also sensed that something more was in him, something inherently decent and good as well. Despite his difficult home life, she soon saw that he had worth. In spite of his doubts and fears, inside him there was much that needed nurturing and caring.

In time, she warmed to him, and they became closer and then inseparable. He noticed that as she accepted him, one especially good thing began to happen. His fears—the gray cloud of his apprehensions—began to disperse. It didn't happen quickly; there were many steps—two forward and one back. But gradually, his days and nights held fewer terrors. It was as though she cured him of his nameless unrest.

As Honey's thoughts about him warmed, her mother's attitude, already frosty, chilled even more. It wasn't difficult to figure why. Here was this disheveled, skinny kid from who-knew-where, sweet-talking one of her beloved daughters just about every night. Her Honey didn't need to take up with some street waif. Worse, Miss Virginia worried that such evening antics would interfere with Honey's schoolwork, once the school year began. The whole thing was disruptive to their well-ordered lives, and she was not going to stand still for it. She didn't go so far as to shoo the boy away from her daughter, but she made it quite obvious that he was as welcome as mold on bread and twice as hard to look at.

For his part, the boy took her attitude in stride. After all, he was used to the cold-shouldering that adults could mete out for hardly any reason; he got enough of that at home. He practiced being oblivious to it and concentrated on making Honey happy. Between his work, music, and a little amateur boxing in his neighborhood (he was a slow-punching paperweight), life was turning out to be better than he ever thought it could be.

His feeling of calmness and normalcy slowly transfigured him. He decided to move from his house, and so he took a room on Calvert Street, eating his meals at restaurants nearby. He felt a serenity like he'd never known. He felt as though he belonged where he was and that even at sixteen, he could fend for himself. He began to grow. Within two years, he stood over six feet tall and weighed 165 pounds. It was like a miracle. No more sideward glances or bigger boys occasional bumping into him. Even the workmen eyed him with some deference. Looking down on his peers did not make him arrogant, though, because he remembered too vividly what being a small boy had felt like, and he wasn't about to inflict that feeling on others.

The Labor Day drum corps competition finally arrived, and the boys, finely arrayed in their brilliant blue-and-white cadet uniforms, prepared for the first of many competitions to come. But those lay in the future. For now, as they entered the huge stadium, even their thoughts got crowded out by hearing the appreciative and supportive roar from the tens of thousands in the stands. The boys from Saint James waited nervously in the stands for their place in the order of performances, and he was taken with the practiced proficiency and expertise of each corps as it strutted through its marching music. It seemed to him that each successive group was somehow better than the one that had just completed. And all performed to a turn, somehow at once brassy, bright, and brilliant.

At last it was their turn. They formed on the periphery of the marching field, and with no more than a nod from their director, they launched into their opening number, stepping crisply, each boy proudly erect and diligently minding his notes, pauses, and stops as they glided over the grassy fields of the stadium. In a few seconds, they were midfield and turned crisply to face the judges in the press booth high above the turf. Their performance progressed without a hitch. They marched and blared their practiced favorites, each in four/four time: "The Colonel Bogey March," then the aria from *Aida*, Sousa's "Washington Post March," and—soon to become the boy's most favorite—"Get Me to the Church on Time."

CHAPTER

3

In their ten-minute performance, the Saint James Drum and Bugle Corps left absolutely nothing on the field. As the last notes of their selection faded, the stadium crowd went wild. Then, still carrying themselves with adult confidence and brisk youthful step, the corps marched from the field, exhilarated that they had accounted well for themselves, their folks, their friends, and their school, though they were shortly to learn that not they but the corps from Hamilton, once again, had finished first and was acclaimed as the champions.

No matter, the boy thought, still awash with excitement, and he made up his mind as they marched out that next year they would trounce all comers.

A year of added maturity had lifted them and instilled confidence in their skills and teamwork, and the very next year, the Drum and Bugle Corps from Saint James, grown poised from their previous strong showing, went on to best all the other corps in the annual competition and were named the champions of Baltimore. Surging with joy, the corps marched from the stadium in flawless formation. Radiating boyish pride and playing their collection of show and martial tunes, they turned smartly east on Thirty-Third Street and paraded back to Saint James. Hundreds of passersby stopped, smiled and applauded; motorists slowed and waved. As they neared the church, Steve glimpsed Honey standing on the sidewalk, her beautiful smile radiant and revealing her obvious pride in him.

The school year opened, a fact of little meaning to him, since he was a worker now and not a class-cutter as before. Academics meant nothing to him except that his time with Honey had to be shortened. Honey took her schoolwork very seriously, a trait more than a little reinforced by her mother. So the time together became more meaningful, and as the weeks and months went by, he began to give serious thought to where all this was taking him. By his fifteenth birthday he came to the realization that the girl—whom he teased had become the center of his existence. Work attracted or repelled him, depending on whether he learned anything useful and new or not. He had left home for good. His home life now was a furnished room, but he was there only to sleep. He still liked to roam, but, now older and smarter, he had curtailed his unauthorized borrowing of vehicles that did not belong to him. Afoot he wandered, but she was never far from his thoughts.

The more he thought of it, the more he came to realize that Honey was the center of his world. She brought with her a certainty about life that conveyed confidence. He felt a reassurance that allowed him to see everything around him with new eyes and to feel that not everything was fearsome and ominous. With her next to him, he gained faith that much of life was good. Maybe they could make their own life together, conforming to no one else's needs but theirs, and their hopes shaped by and for them—for each other.

It was then that he made up his mind that they would be together. They both were so young, yet he knew that he had never felt such feelings before and that they were genuine and real, as real as the air he breathed. Working, walking together, sitting side by side in a crowded theater, laughing, and walking hand in hand—all these simple things and more were better because he was with her. He was hers, and she was his.

The routine of his life, once drably predictable and devoid of laughter, picked up its pace. Days raced by, then weeks. He existed now to finish his workday, rush to his room, scrub, eat, and then be off like a shot to see her, at least on the school nights when her mother allowed it. Weekends were made for her and became milestones, each with laughter and fun. For once he felt like a child and not a fugitive who dodged classes, cops, or anyone who might interfere in his forays.

He was fast maturing into a lanky, tall adolescent. He and Honey became one couple among a circle of other teens who did not lack for fun, though none of them hailed from affluence—their fathers were men who worked with their hands and brought home modest wages. Yet all their circle could find amusement in the simplest pleasures. For a hayride they rented a truck, filled it with the grassy golden fodder, and leaped aboard; the oldest drove them through and around the city. They went to the fancier movie houses, the ones downtown that had plush velvet seats and popcorn still steaming in its bag. They took the trolley car to Dundalk and enjoyed a swimming hole there—a place where they could be kids and splash each other and laugh—and then returned on the trolley, all of them happy and spent. There were roller skating parties at a rink on North Avenue and eating out occasionally at a place on Loch Raven Boulevard, where people ate in their cars, with the food served to them by girls on skates. Each weekend there were CYO dances, some at Saint James and some at Saint John, two blocks farther. Although he perhaps did not realize it then, the time was idyllic, made more so in his memory.

As he grew in height, he got stronger. Working with his father was not physically strenuous, but the more he grew, he longed to be free from his father. His absence from that household was a trigger to the older man, but the boy would not tell his father where he had moved. That decision, like the place, was his, at least as long as he could make the rent payment each week. His dad tried in vain to find the place. The room he rented, like his decision to live there, the boy felt, was his new life. And they were his *own*. Child or not, he felt that because he worked and made his way, he owned the right to be to himself, shedding forever the hard looks and perpetual chorus of complaints at his parents' home.

Young Steve wanted man's work—building, lifting, learning new things. He gravitated toward construction and got a job with the Chew Company, building new apartments. It was fast-paced, but the older men took the time to explain to the boy what each task entailed. He was quick to learn. In no time, he was pulling lead pipes into the unfinished walls of each unit. It was hard work, and it gratified him. But often on the job site, there were moments when he got stymied—when he unable to read the information necessary for a complex install, or when he could not calculate the lengths to which each segment had to be cut. It was his skipped school classes coming home to trouble him again, not the first of what would prove to be many future times.

The months flew by and melded into years. He celebrated his seventeenth birthday, and his hopes for Honey grew and merged with his new belief in himself. He recognized that he was maturing into a calmer, more rational man and that Honey had instilled his faith in himself.

It was not an especially auspicious evening, merely one of their pleasant interludes between school nights. He took her hand and looked into her eyes. "Would you consider marrying me?" he asked. It was unexpected, unrehearsed; touchingly plain-spoken, and totally real.

She didn't blink. "Yes." She said it quietly, as though he should have known the answer without ever having asked the question. Like that, they committed to each other and cemented themselves forever closer. There was more than love between them; there was trust—trust that all that lay ahead of them would be well.

At age eighteen, he needed parental permission to marry. His father was adamant in his refusal—*under no circumstances*—and that led to heated words. Steve retorted that he was prepared to run off, if that's what it would take, but he referred the issue to a higher authority: his grandfather.

When Pop weighed in, there was, as ever, even-handed reasoning. He saw that the boy knew his own mind. "The boy means well. He plans to do it proper—in a church wedding." The old man was adamant with his adult son regarding the future of his oldest grandson. "You *are* going to give him your permission," Pop said quietly to his son. Steve's father was trumped and finally relented.

The happy couple was married in Saint John's Church. Along with the well-wishers, however, various voices predicted the quick demise of their marriage, almost before the vows had been spoken. Both were eighteen. Steve and Honey ignored the predictions and happily rented an apartment on Claremont Avenue in northeast Baltimore. The year was 1948.

Steve knew that marriage and being a husband meant that any growing up he needed to do had to be done fast. Upon his shoulders lay the responsibility to support himself and his cherished new wife. But he was not unduly concerned; after all, he had supported himself these past years. He was a good worker, even if the printed word or some numbers gave him pause. Yet the job sites demanded that his reading improve, and it did, over time—slowly, through determination, memorization of the look of the words, and maybe a bit of osmosis.

"Just bring home a paycheck every week," Honey had said, "and we'll be all right."

But that was the problem with construction work; it was all or nothing. As jobs ended, there were inevitable layoffs, not a good situation for any marriage but especially not for a new one. He needed steady work, so he found a good job at the Baltimore Trolley Company as a mechanic's helper in the bus shop.

Two years after their wedding, their first baby arrived—a little girl, Sondra. In the hospital waiting room, Steve began to fully comprehend the seriousness of what was occurring. Honey's mother studied the worry etched on his features and, probably for the first time, truly realized that there was much more to this young man than she'd ever imagined. It was an anxious day for both but one that brought them closer.

Then he was a father. He made a promise to himself that he would never raise his children as he had been raised. He would raise them with support and soft-spoken encouragement, with gentleness, and with love.

When they brought the baby home, there was no separate room for her in their small apartment. She slept in a crib next to their bed. The first nights he was afraid to drift off. He lay awake, listening for the sound of her breathing, fearing something bad might frighten or seize her. It was anxiety but for reasonable cause. He felt like most new fathers, that he could not be derelict in his protection of her. She was a helpless infant, and she was his.

Honey took to motherhood as though the skills were known to her since birth. In a way, spending days and nights with her mother, a single parent raising three children, Honey had intuitively absorbed the lessons of motherhood, and she emulated her mother in so many of the ways of caring for and nurturing her precious little girl.

Once the young couple was accustomed to parenthood, things settled into a comfortable if hectic routine. As with most couples following the war, they decided that Honey would be the homemaker, and Steve would continue as the breadwinner. In short order, baby Sondra was walking and then attempting to talk. Steve and Honey were a happy couple, now turning twenty. Honey was pregnant again, and in 1952, their son, Stephen, was born. Even as an infant, he was a brawny, healthy boy. The months and years began to fly by.

Not long after the birth of Stephen, the trolley company was struck by the Transit Workers Union. Mechanical workers were locked out until settlement could be reached, and Steve's work—and paychecks—stopped. Following the strike, efficiency experts were brought in who recommended fewer bus shop employees. Many of the workers faced layoffs or assignments as drivers. Steve made a bid to be a trolley driver and he was once again earning a paycheck to care for his family. He was twenty-five by then, and, like any man, he was beginning to wonder where all his work was leading him.

The trolley cars conveyed tens of thousands of people each day. Quaint conveyances, they rode rails that crisscrossed Baltimore, carried more passengers than modern buses, and were powered by electricity transmitted through dual connectors extending above the vehicle to overhead wires. In the winter, each first car out of the barn was equipped with a modified plow affixed to its front end. Snow accumulation on the tracks was easily plowed and the tracks cleared for all cars that followed.

But the threat of layoffs spurred Steve. Such a situation simply would not do. Even infrequent periods without money coming in was a major obstacle. In their four years of marriage, the couple had saved barely anything. They lived from one payday to the next, and any interruption in that flow of money was a serious issue. After much discussion, Steve and Honey decided that working for any company that offered poor job security and no benefits was not a good future for them and their growing family. Soon after, with Sondra in tow, he ventured downtown to the City Hall where a jobs bulletin board directed possible employees to a veritable half wall of employment notices by city agencies. Diligently he copied down the requirements of every posted job notice: public works, the fire department, sanitation, and one listing openings with the police department. He decided to apply to all of them, no matter the nature of the work, the location, or hours. All offered what he sought: regular work and paychecks, health benefits, and a pension after thirty or more years of service.

But all listed eight completed school grades as an essential. That was a problem. A big one.

Within a week Steve got a positive response. It was from the police department. He would begin the police academy classes in July, so he quit his job as a trolley driver. Shortly thereafter, he received another letter from the police department stating that the schedule had changed and that classes would not start until October. This presented an unexpected time between paychecks, so Steve landed a job driving a cab to bring in some money. The irony of the situation didn't escape his notice. Him—a cop. His father would not believe that his oldest son might just be ready to change his life around for the good.

Honey Dolores Margaret
Varley - 16 years old

Stephen Bernard Tabeling
III - 16 years old

Steve and Honey's Wedding
Day - May 8, 1948

Honey, Sondra, Steve IV
Patti, "little" Honey and Steve III
1958

CHAPTER

4

On his first day at his new job, Steve found himself with forty-nine other men in a room rigged out as a classroom on the second floor of the Baltimore Police Academy. The institution occupied space in the Northern District in a historic Victorian-era structure, built and occupied long before motor vehicles existed.

As new trainees, they were expected to act respectably, and they shuffled across the polished vintage linoleum floors quietly and without causing a stir. As they filed quietly up the antique staircase into the old classroom, Steve felt a familiar surge of emotion return—equal parts panic (at being confined in a room full of strangers) and tedium (as though his grade school years had returned to taunt him). His fears were real; most of these young men had high school diplomas, and most had left good jobs, some as office workers and some from factories and plants. Many were veterans; they had been places and seen and done things he could only guess at. How would he ever keep up with such men? He was twenty-five and could barely read and write. His arithmetic skills were even worse than that. Although it was October, the unventilated room felt stifling. He thought, darkly, that maybe this move had been a big mistake.

The hiring had not gone smoothly either. Told by the department that his class would start in July, he had resigned his job but then was informed there were not enough to form a new class. Meanwhile, the money that he and Honey needed to get by had ceased. In desperation, he became a cabbie, hauling passengers through and around the city.

He also had needed to address his dearth of an eighth-grade completion certificate. Grimly, he enrolled in equivalency classes at Baltimore City College, a public high school housed in a huge granite edifice, perched atop a hill overlooking Thirty-Third Street. Once there, his classroom angst flooded back, weighted by the utter inadequacy he felt in a classroom. But he vowed to make the most of the opportunity—he had no choice.

The classroom work was very hard for him. Though he was listed as having finished seven grades, by no stretch had he *successfully* completed them. There were too many skipped days, missed exams, and failure to comprehend. The significant factor was that schools teach and people learn on a progressive basis; each new year builds on the skills gained in the prior year. The reality of his unruliness as a child relegated him to owning a series of disjointed and apparently unrelated facts in a variety of disciplines. There had been precious little progressive anything because there was hardly any foundation on which to build it.

Still, it was something he simply had to do. Asking questions helped, and the teacher contributed her knowledge, insight, and patience. And there was the fact that he only had to pass a test, though it was going to be a bear. After that, he reasoned, he could jettison whatever of the studies clouded his mind and get on with life.

Honey helped. As she did with all things that she did for her family, she sensed the dread within her husband and patiently repeated the points he needed to master. Math was the worst because it is the most progressive of academics. Patiently she drilled him in the times tables, long division, fractions, decimals, and percentages. Nothing about math came easily for him. English grammar wasn't much better, but as he struggled, it began to come to him.

On the day of the test, he was weak-kneed with anticipation and dread. As the monitor handed out the booklets, Steve quietly took his and awaited the direction to begin. He thought he could hear his heart pounding as he opened the booklet.

Several weeks later he received a letter informing him that he had passed. Then it was on to the Baltimore Police Department.

The academy instructors cycled through their classes—most of them were subject-matter experts who purportedly were good at what they did in the police department, which was fine for them, he reasoned, because they certainly were not very good at teaching. They droned, showing little enthusiasm and less patience, as they held forth on a litany of subjects: the organization of the department, its history and traditions, traffic enforcement procedures, first aid, and many more. More than once he felt his head begin to droop but caught himself and pushed himself to sit erect in his seat, hoping none of the others had noticed. When he glanced around furtively, he saw some of the others fighting to stay awake as well.

The man who taught law was a lieutenant, a balding and rotund man with thinning white hair and a plodding delivery. He rarely altered his vocal pitch or volume as he read the essential elements of each crime from his *Digest of Criminal Laws*. "Larceny," he announced, "is the taking and carrying away of the property of another, with the intent to deprive that person permanently thereof." At this he might glance up to scan the lake of bored expressions before him. Occasionally, he would ad lib. "Note there has to be *asportation*; that is, the act of carrying off the thing or property taken."

His name was Otto Urban. Years earlier he had chased a troublemaker not far from his home and had been shot. While recovering, he had been assigned to the academy, where he was to instruct generations of new police officers in the law.

Very rarely, he ventured into humor. "Mopery," he told his students, "is the act of exhibiting oneself nude in the presence of a blind woman." He did this to gauge what percentage of the trainees had stayed with him to that point. Noting that, he continued, in his monotone, to detail all the elements of statutory and common law.

Several weeks into the program, the trainees were brought to the indoor pistol range to begin what would prove to be a grueling regimen for some of them. Safe and efficient operation of the six-shot revolver—ideally, a *mastery* of the deadly weapon they would carry throughout their careers—was a prerequisite to successful completion of academy training. The cavernous shooting facility was dark and forbidding, particularly to students who had never before used a firearm—Steve had never even *held* a firearm. Ear protection was not furnished, and the deafening crack of each round as it was discharged, grossly intensified by the confined space, bordered on pain-inducing.

Once the lectures on safe and efficient operation of the weapon were completed in an adjacent classroom, the recruits filed into the range space and lined up as directed, each in a shooting position twenty-five feet from a fresh paper target. As directed, each loaded and holstered the weapon. On command, each drew his pistol, rigidly extended his gun hand, aimed by aligning the rear and front sights, and then gently squeezed off two rounds. The instructor's whistle signaled them to stop and re-holster the weapon. A second whistle directed them to repeat the process twice more.

After several relays, the targets were returned via overhead tracks to each shooter's position for review. The range instructors examined each sheet and advised each shooter what improvements he needed to make in his stance, grip, or trigger pull. Except for a few holes in its upper right corner, and a few strays, Steve's target looked nearly new. From that day forward, he spent his lunchtimes in the gym, balancing a penny on the front sight of his revolver—an assignment designed to focus the rookie's concentration on mastering his sight picture and, especially, acquiring a silky-smooth trigger pull. Snapping the trigger roughly caused the weapon to veer off target, signaled by the penny tumbling to the hardwood floor of the gymnasium. It was humbling, but, as in all things, Steve made up his mind to do, and it got him into the groove of shooting. Soon, he was hitting what he aimed at.

After weapons qualification, the recruits were assigned to radio cars on the weekends to acclimate them to what they might encounter on the streets of Baltimore. Each trainee was issued a handgun and holster before departing the academy for the weekend. Although they were armed when they worked these details, they wore civilian attire.

The thought of entering people's houses turned up his senses a notch. Steve thought of the possibility of facing a man with a weapon. What would he do about a spousal assault. Domestic altercations were common. Steve saw first-hand how domestic arguments were handled by veteran officers. What would he do if the decision was his. Many of the routine calls were charged with the potential for violence; many of the residents openly disparaged the officers, as if defying them. One in particular stayed with him. "He won't let me do what I want," a woman screamed as the officers entered. "He's suffocatin' me!"

The veteran cop sighed and eyed both the husband and wife. The husband's voice, which a second earlier had reverberated from the sidewalk, was now subdued. "What she wants is to run the streets," he insisted. "Well, screw her. Let her run. Go on; get on out!"

The officer stood calmly between the two to reduce the chance for violence. He said impassively to the man, "That's how you feel?" The man nodded. The officer turned to the woman. "You too?" he said evenly. When she nodded, he instructed both of them to place their right hands on his badge.

"Okay," he said. "By virtue of the authority vested in me as a peace officer in the city of Baltimore, state of Maryland, I hereby grant you a final decree of divorce." He turned to the man and concluded the "ceremony" with a nod toward the front door. "This her place, is it? Then you get your things and find a place to live because you're done here, okay? Go on now."

Without a murmur the man did as he was told. Case closed.

As the weekend details progressed, Steve was struck by the contrast in the officers. Some, sharply turned out in their uniforms, were quite efficient. They were well informed of the conditions within their bailiwicks—supervisory sectors patrolled by a number of officers—and conversant with pertinent laws. Others appeared diffident, bored, or simply uninterested in the "job," as they referred to it, or anything about the job. Many were horrified at the prospect of shepherding a rookie anywhere and made no secret of their contempt for the fledgling cops.

Steve's insecurities did not lessen with continued exposure to the job; indeed, his fears were magnified. He dreaded the prospect of writing reports; he was barely literate and had never written anything even as complex as a letter. His knowledge of grammar was uncertain at best; his spelling was even more suspect. Each night after class, academy staff sent the trainees home with ten new words to master: their spellings and definitions. Honey, who had excelled in schoolwork, sat with him at their kitchen table, hearing him recite his words. With her patience and in time the words became imbedded.

By graduation, he breathed easier, secure that he had weathered this most difficult classroom work, though in years to come he often thought he had learned precious little that was of use to him in working a district. But he had earned a certificate of successful completion—his first ever gotten through classroom effort—though he was about to learn how little he had learned, foremost being that classroom traumas were the least of the traumas that might befall a working cop. As his career kicked off, he soon realized there were far worse things in the world than boring classroom lectures.

After graduation he was assigned to the Northwestern District annex, so-called because it abutted the northwestern corner of the parent district. There, the neighborhoods enjoyed wide avenues, tree-lined streets, a scenic man-built lake, and parks flanked by wide rowhouses with broad verandas. The people were upper middle class—doctors, dentists, jewelers, bankers; Baltimore's professional elite. They were mostly affluent or soon-to-be, and they largely abstained from police services, so calls were few. Calls for service came by way of call boxes, those ubiquitous cast-iron structures housing telephones, strategically placed throughout the city. Additional and separate high poles sporting lights were mounted every few blocks; when the light flashed its amber glow, the officer knew to quickly proceed to the nearest call box. His services were needed.

Steve was assigned to foot patrol. His first days wearing the uniform and badge filled him with apprehension. He was troubled not so much by the prospect of injury as by making a stupid mistake and embarrassing himself or the other cops. He wore his new uniform, purchased via payroll deductions at two dollars per paycheck. For each shift, he dutifully trudged from one corner of his foot post to another, hoping for a call.

The neighborhoods that graced the annex were mostly peaceful, and he was largely disappointed. In no time, he was bored and asked to be sent to a busier place. His request was granted, and he soon found himself in west Baltimore in neighborhoods surrounding Pennsylvania Avenue, a commercial artery that boasted the best in black entertainment, eateries, and theaters. It was the cultural mecca for the city's blacks. He quickly learned he would be bored no more.

A rookie officer was like an invisible man to his sergeants and often even to the public. As for the older officers, they made no bones about avoiding him as though he was diseased. Quite often a veteran officer would cross the street rather than encounter a stupid, just-from-the-academy officer. Rookies, the veterans believed, were unlucky, clumsy, and uppity to boot, and they asked too many stupid questions. They were generally regarded as unwelcome pairs of eyes and ears.

Steve's anxiety over writing continued to eat at him. Then one night, his nightmare came true—he got a call for service that required a police report. He was beside himself. In mounting desperation, he did the unthinkable: He used the call box to call for his sergeant. Some supervisors of that era discouraged any and all such calls. Only serious things needed to intrude on their privacy: murders and the like. For all else, they expected not to be bothered by mortals.

As his sergeant pulled up to him, he cranked down his window slightly and inquired curtly as to the reason for being disturbed. As the disconcerted Tabeling confessed his need for assistance with writing the report, the supervisor gruffly interrupted him and instructed the wretched rookie to place his hand over his badge. "Feel that?" the sergeant asked. "That means you are a *police* officer." Window cranked up, he sped away.

It was winter, and Steve walked the concrete sidewalks clad in a heavy knee-length woolen overcoat that made any movement, particularly quick movement, difficult. Worse, the issued weapon he carried, a Colt .38 special revolver, was worn on a gun belt beneath the outer garment and was challenging to draw from its holster at any time but especially in a stressful situation. There also was the fact that police officers were not issued handcuffs, though a few officers purchased their own. It was a safety issue, yet Steve felt that such an expense took food off the family table.

Thus, to make an arrest away from a call box—and most arrests were that way—entailed approaching the subject and ordering him to turn around and then apprising him that his freedom to move about was about to be revoked. It was good practice at that point to firmly latch on to the subject's belt and march him to the call box. Once there, the officer needed to withdraw his bronze call-box key, an outsized relic of an earlier era; fit it into the large keyhole; turn and open the iron door; and then call communications to request a transporting wagon. If all went well, this was done expeditiously. If, however, the subject objected to being arrested, as frequently occurred, the officer had no recourse but to struggle with, wrestle, box, tug, punch, and otherwise physically convince the arrestee that cooperation was the sensible solution to their mutual problem, while hoping that a concerned citizen had summoned some help. With two or more suspects, it could get far worse. As an effective arrest procedure, much was lacking. None of this took into consideration the possibility that friends of the arrested person might intervene to free the arrestee or merely to beat the officer senseless. Officer Tabeling learned quickly that there was a wide range of possibilities when dealing with volatile people in strained circumstances and that many of them had unpleasant possible outcomes. The best course of action was for him to approach all situations with his senses sharp and ready for almost anything.

He learned that walking a foot post, usually about a three-by-four-block area, put him in contact with dozens of people each day, and some of them shared information, though to them it might be a bit of gossip, a rumor, something someone else had seen and told them. And these seemingly insignificant snippets could be stitched together in the mind of the officer until a pattern might emerge, like a paint-by-numbers picture or an embroidered bedspread. Might be a lot of nonsense; might be something useful. Regardless, he was quick to store the info passed to him and let the facts marinate in his brain. It was the first job where he was expected to *think*.

It was a job that afforded a man the opportunity to do some good. Many of the residents were impoverished, the result of alcohol, ill health, drugs, or bad breaks. Some had served time in prison, which made their potential for work problematic. The children affected him especially; he noticed that many of them obviously did not get enough to eat. Around Christmas that year he made it his business to convince several local grocers to chip in. A bit here, a little there, and they assembled baskets of food for the neediest families. Delivering them did much more good for him, he realized.

Foot patrol imparted a freedom, very much like his grammar school days. Essentially, he was free to roam his post—or posts, for quite often a shortage of officers required him to work two or more adjoining areas. Fine by him.

He got scant on-the-job training from supervisors or veteran officers, but he was free to learn on his own. This entailed risks, not of physical harm as much as administrative peril. Stepping on the wrong set of toes could get you moved in a hurry. Or disciplined. Often, as he rotated assignments between and among posts, he worked some areas with pawn shops grouped along commercial areas. He was quick to learn they could be a gold mine of information.

The owners were required to keep logs of property brought in for collateral, noting the item, a thorough description, the date, the cash value it had fetched, and the name of the person pawning the item. Included as well were notes that described the redemption of an item.

Steve began to understand that his mind worked better the more he stretched it and that he had something pretty close to a photographic memory. Of course, the pawnshop information was only half of the equation. He reasoned that if he scanned the police district's burglary and larceny reports, he might spot commonalities—such as that the diamond ring pawned on the third of the month by Joe Burglar was the same half carat marquis set in white gold piece that was listed as taken in a home burglary on the second.

The more he made search-and-comparisons, the more he saw connections. He encouraged the pawnshop owner to call him if anyone came in to redeem a certain piece, a courtesy that much benefited the owner, as his licensing depended on his absolute cooperation with the police.

Soon he had the process honey smooth. Why chase after the shadows of burglars, he thought, when, with a little imagination and a bit of work, the burglars would come to him? Burglary arrests were felony arrests and considered good work, especially for a new officer. The workload kept him busy, and for that he was grateful. For once in his young life, he felt that he was doing something that mattered.

One night he received a call to "investigate the trouble" at a house nearby. As he hurried to the location, a radio car sped past him with its dome light flashing. As Steve arrived at the address, he saw that both he and the officer in the radio car had been dispatched to the call. When he knocked on the door, a male voice from inside told them to come in. Officer Tabeling observed at once that a male was sitting quietly on a chair; next to him was the body of a woman, drenched in blood and obviously deceased. On the floor in front of the passive man lay a revolver. Tabeling inspected the weapon and saw that one of the six cylinders held only the shell casing.

"I had enough of her shit," the man said calmly. The two officers made the notifications, called for the morgue wagon, searched the scene, and took the man into custody. What was remarkable was that, as open and shut as it was, such a thing was not uncommon in the new district where he worked. Cultural center or not, the area was besieged by violence—cuttings, shootings, rapes.

Not many weeks after that, he was summoned to the captain's office. While speculating what he had done wrong, he knocked on the door and entered. "Yes, sir," he said. "You wanted to see me?"

The captain, a district commander who noticed good police work when he saw or heard of it, patted him on the back. "You've got initiative, Officer. I see all you're doing out there. I want you on my plainclothes squad. I need you to start right away. That be okay?"

And, of course the new cop with two years on the job thought it'd be just fine. The job involved investigating all serious crimes in the district, including murders. It was a plum opportunity and nearly too good to be true. He couldn't wait to tell Honey. She beamed with pride. "For the first time, I'll be able to think and solve problems. I should have been doing this all along, since I turned twenty-one. For the first time since I started working, I get to use my brain."

CHAPTER

5

S uccess at police work is contingent upon good luck, and that is problematic, though good cops will tell anyone who asks that good luck—or any luck—is often proportionate to the number of hours a cop is willing to work at something. Hard work often draws success to it.

Tabeling's new partner was many years his senior. Charlie Scroogs was a short pleasant officer with thinning white hair, who had a determination to succeed in the district investigator role. Truth was, he had something to prove, having been booted out of the downtown holdup squad for an indiscretion. Consigned to the purgatory that was the west side of town, he brought determination and finely honed investigative skills to the two-man unit, as well as a solid work ethic. He was the kind of man who wouldn't give up easily. Those attributes meshed nicely with Tabeling's outlook: *Keep at it until you get it*. The two men promptly bonded.

With no time for formal training, they learned on the run about the cast of local thugs as they moved from one crime scene to the next. Their police district, which eventually was renamed Western District, held boatloads of opportunities for two ambitious cops, each one determined to prove himself to the captain as well as to his new partner.

To enhance their odds of success, they consulted regularly with the robbery detectives downtown who worked west-side crimes. Scanning those reports gave them insight into the tendencies of each gang or individual who committed violent street crimes, learning their weaponry, for instance, their mode of approach, favorite targets, mannerisms, dress, descriptions, and method of escape. That way, the two investigators could anticipate things. Any advantage was a step closer to clearing crimes and locking up the criminals who did them.

An early case was a number of robberies involving gangs of men armed with revolvers. They were businesslike; it was get the money and get gone. They seemed to understand that less time at a holdup ensured less (or no) time in prison. Tabeling studied the descriptions and then reinterviewed victims, some of whom recalled that one of the holdup men wore green suede shoes, an uncommon footwear, especially in that part of town. The partners began making the rounds of bars and pool halls, interviewing mostly uncooperative patrons but always with their senses keen—it wasn't out of the ordinary for two white cops to get attacked and stomped, just 'cause it was the thing to do.

Then one afternoon, as the pair entered a pool hall on the Avenue, Tabeling spotted Mr. Green Shoes and pulled him aside. The two officers invited him to the district for a chat. With a cop on either side of him, he couldn't refuse.

With more than three years invested in the job, Tabeling had become engrossed by the art and science of questioning and interrogation. He recognized the critical significance of getting a suspect to open up and let the investigator inside his head. Whenever he had the chance, he eavesdropped when another cop sat down with a suspect. Tabeling watched as the officer invariably told the man to seat himself. Then the process began with a barrage of questions, such as "Where exactly were you last Saturday night?" Or "What can you tell me about such-and-such yoking that happened on Mosher at Lafayette last Wednesday?"

Tabeling saw that the proof of efficiency was in how well the interview approaches worked—how much relevant and useable information was revealed. After a number of fly-on-the-wall observations, he began to see that most of the approaches were wide of the mark, for rarely did a streetwise thug cave in to an occasional slap alongside the head. The cop tough-guy act worked even worse. It made no sense to try to out-tough-guy these guys because all of them hailed from dangerous neighborhoods and crushed families—father gone and momma in jail. They were living lives where violence rose like the sun each day and stayed out like the moon, each and every night. Most white cops could not comprehend. Even the youngest of the suspects was used to the threat of violence; it was part of his neighborhood's family tree. It was gouged and drilled in innumerable walls, autos, and staircases like the countless bullet holes that marked his world. A gunshot in the night was an ordinary occurrence, and nobody even looked up or looked out to see what it was. It stained the streets and sidewalks; old blood puddles, dried in a day but there all the same. So to risk what might happen to him if he ratted out a brother to please a cop? Well, just say no way. "I'll run the risk. Just go on and talk yourself out, Officer, and then put me in the cell."

The more Tabeling considered it the more he realized they were people—different in outlooks and locales and prospects, to be sure, but people all the same. *No man I ever met,* he reasoned, *reacts well to threats. Just the opposite. Maybe that's their wiring. Maybe the wiring makes them dig in deeper when they get jammed.*

Tabeling was not a theory man; he was a tried-it-and-failed man and then a try-something-else man. After a while, something else came to him—no tough guy approach.

"Good morning," he said. "Why don't you have a seat? I'm Officer Tabeling. This is my partner, Officer Scroogs. That's right; have a seat right there. We want to ask you some questions. But listen, did you see that game last night? Can you believe one guy can drop that many balls in nine innings?" Tabeling laughed, and Mr. Green Shoes was taken aback. He was used to being yanked off the street and brought inside, like this police station. He shifted gears and stared back and then seemed to calm a bit.

"Yeah," he said genially, "my granny fields baseballs better than that." He was offered a coffee but declined. "Give me the jitters," he said.

They proceeded in that congenial vein for a few minutes, with Tabeling closely observing the man's mannerisms and body language but all the while exuding professional yet affable vibes. "You married?" he asked. "Got any sisters or brothers? Yeah? How many? How do you get along with them?"

Green Shoes was keeping up. So far this was a different breed of cat, this cop, and he stared at Tabeling like he was studying him as well. "I'm oldest of four. I don't see none of them much. One is dead. One is in Carolina. We ain't close."

Tabeling listened intently and then said, "You know we're looking at some stuff that's been happening around here and wonder if you can help. We hear that you know everybody anybody needs to know. People we're looking for … well, they been holding people up with guns. Truth is, you match a couple descriptions we got. We wanted to talk to you about these holdups." Tabeling held a stack of reports and placed them on the table. "This one on the top was last Wednesday. Two men with guns. The steakhouse bar and restaurant on the Avenue." He held his hand up to shush the man if he felt compelled to talk. "No need to say it wasn't you; we got two people said they saw you. Spotted your fine-looking footwear. Plus, we know who the leader of your gang is. Got him two rooms down. And he is talking to the detectives as we speak."

"Leader?" Mr. Green Shoes sputtered. "What leader would that be?"

"Uh," Tabeling responded slowly, "that would be a Mr. Willie White. You know him, I think? 'Cause he certainly seems to know you."

Tabeling watched as the man lost control of his body language. Leaning forward, leaning back, listing to left, then right, he was fast losing his practiced poise. "White?" he said. "*Mister* Willie White?

Well, let me say Mr. Willie White could not lead me to a charity whorehouse; not Willie White. He a fool; can't dodge himself. Plan stickups? Ridiculous. Who do you think has the what-it-takes to spot a good spot—not too busy early in the day? Get in. Get the money. Get out. Nobody hurt. Be gone when the police get there? Long gone. Who?" he asked with some vehemence.

Tabeling sat impassively, scrawling longhand notes and shaking his head. "Who would that be?"

"Well, I can tell you who it ain't," the man erupted. "'Cause that fool can't tie his own shoes without help. Me, that's who! Me! I did all that."

"Oh?" Officer Tabeling said quietly. "You? I see."

Charlie and Steve glanced up at each other. Charlie nodded, a faint smile on his face.

Except for the details of victims, places, faces, amounts, dates and times—work for which Charlie and now Steve apparently were put on the west side to perform—they were done. Each time it happened, it was different yet strangely similar. *Be polite; no raising the voice or slamming things.* These weren't strengths; they only showed weakness. *Be courteous; you are dealing with a person—different upbringing, different values but a person all the same.* Most cared about loved ones, especially their mothers, aunts, and grannies. And most responded to some modicum of reason, as in "you can help us with these three west-side holdups, and we can help you so that you don't go away for a hundred years."

And oddly, no matter how badass they were or thought they were, most responded to courtesy with the same. Maybe it was because they didn't want to look shabby. Maybe they actually valued the humanness. Steve recognized that he was learning the techniques that worked through much trial and error and patience and not giving up—and convincing suspects of two things: (1) he knew *more* about them than they could imagine; and (2) he actually listened and cared about what they thought.

The trick was to find out if he was dealing with a leader—a firstborn of multiple children, for example, who was used to telling little brothers and sisters what to do. He could not try to overpower someone who considered himself a leader. That was absolutely the wrong approach. Once Tabeling was able to establish to the suspect that *he* was also a leader, the suspect wanted to live up to Tabeling's expectations, even if he faced prison time.

And deep down, all of them wanted to tell somebody how smart, brave, and nimble they were. Because deep down, everybody wants to tell his story.

As the weeks passed, Steve learned that the west side never lacked for colorful and creative crooks. There was a gang of juveniles who robbed motorists stopped at red lights—they skated up to the victim's vehicle on both sides. One diverted the driver's attention long enough for his partner to smash the passenger-side window, grab property from the front seat, and skate off. Then one day, they skated into the arms of the police.

Tabeling made sure to familiarize himself and Charlie with new wrinkles like that in every suspect's mode of operation. Responding to a holdup in progress, both officers knew from study that the holdup man usually fled north, using the closest alley that got him instantly out of anybody's line of sight. He would run one or two blocks at full speed—Tabeling believed there were world-class sprinters out there who could have competed in the Olympics—and then turn, usually westbound on a narrow side street, and jog off.

But one crook they studied, after having made a clean getaway, inexplicably filtered himself back to the crime scene to check on police response, police presence, witnesses—who knew? Figuring out that tactic helped Steve and Charlie to be there waiting for him upon his return.

The days never lacked for action—follow-ups, canvasses of the neighborhoods, witness location, occasional warrant service—nor did either man lack for extra money, thanks to court attendance, for example. District court paid a princely three dollars, no matter if a cop only sat there for four hours, waiting to testify. It was three dollars regardless. Downtown court paid five dollars and was often an all-day ordeal, but it was extra money, always welcome in a growing family.

Steve's daughter Sondra was then in second grade at Saint Mary's. She was a lovely girl and, like her mother, a very good student. Their baby boy, Stephen, was four, and he promised to be an athlete. Even so young, he threw a tennis ball with unerring accuracy. Little Dolores, not remarkably also called Honey, was next in line and was a gregarious, precocious, and energetic child. When she was dressed up to go somewhere special, Steve and Honey knew to take her picture, for the instant she got close to their backyard, signs of play would quickly adorn her formerly pristine dress. Patty, the youngest, had a sweet disposition but was a worrier. As a infant she developed asthma and a skin disorder, and both parents fretted over her discomfort. No doctor who saw her seemed able to ease her suffering.

Then one day while on patrol, Tabeling saw a thug brutally punch a woman in the face, knock her to the sidewalk, snatch her purse, and quickly scamper away. Tabeling followed. Without a radio, as often happened, he was unable to get help. The accepted way to summon assistance if nothing else was possible was to fire his weapon once in the air and hope it attracted nearby officers, but he realized that if he slowed to do that, he might lose sight of the crook.

The man sprinted from the street into the railroad yard near the city jail, and, for an instant, Tabeling did lose sight of him. He crouched as he ran alongside the freight cars and inspected the underside of each, determined to find the man.

Perhaps he bent too low as he checked under each car because from nowhere, a fist launched from underneath the car and cracked Tabeling squarely on the jaw, knocking him on his back and very nearly knocking him out. He had found the thug. Tabeling fought to regain full consciousness and feared he might again lose the man. He reached up as the man hovered over him and did the only thing he could think to do to regain the situation—he grabbed the man by the testicles and, with an iron grip toughened by years of construction, crushed them.

Awkward though it might have looked, it worked very well. Tabeling now had a very effective come-along. The man's shrieks of agony were audible enough to attract a pair of officers, who got there and chuckled at the sight. The suspect had ceased resisting.

Later, as he located the woman who had been attacked, he interviewed her at her place of employment, which happened to be a dermatologist's office. He discovered she was the medical secretary. Obviously grateful for Tabeling's decisive and quick arrest, the doctor said, "I know you can't take a reward, though you certainly deserve one. But if I can ever be of assistance to you or your family, I want you to avail yourself of my services."

Some weeks later after examining and testing Patty, the doctor was able to formulate an original salve that effectively and permanently cured the little girl's skin problem. One good turn had nurtured another.

That year, to house their growing family, they bought a spacious home in a nice neighborhood. It was their first. All his young life, Tabeling had prayed for a good wife and healthy children and a home. It was the reassuring love he had always craved. He was whole, then, because of them.

Things were coming together nicely in the police department as well. Tabeling and Charlie got to be known as energetic and prolific investigators who found bad guys and put them away. Steve had taken the sergeant's examination months before—and a devilishly difficult test it had been. Walking away from the testing site, he put the matter out of his head, thinking it had been a waste of his time.

Then one day, without warning, he was summoned to the captain's office. To his amazement, as he entered he recognized the police commissioner, Bernard Schmidt, who smiled and extended his hand.

"Congratulations, Officer," the commissioner said. "You're going to be a sergeant. Tomorrow morning. See you then."

Steve was both speechless and elated. Promotion to sergeant would bring a sizeable raise in pay, a fact not to be discounted, not with a wife and four children to feed. "Thank you, sir," he said, and the commissioner, who seemed to be enjoying the moment more than Tabeling, smiled broadly at him. With the nicest part of his job completed, Schmidt departed.

Tabeling was euphoric, an unfamiliar but welcome sensation. He knew Honey and the kids would be proud of him. He thought of his father for an instant and pictured that stern, hardworking man with his sour expression. *Maybe,* Steve thought, *this'll make him proud too. Imagine.*

But the day was young, and he left the station to resume patrol. Promotion or not, he was still being paid to do police work. He scanned the area as he and Charlie walked, and not far from the stationhouse, he peripherally glimpsed a man, bound and gagged and awkwardly hopping up a staircase that led from the basement of a corner house. When the man saw the two police officers, he freed one hand and pointed east.

Charlie and Steve sped in that direction. Tabeling had the feeling the robber might backtrack, using the alleys to approach unseen. As he neared the first of the east/west alleys, he drew back. He realized that if his sixth sense was correct, he'd better be ready. Without hesitation, he drew his weapon and stepped quickly to the alley entrance. There, not twenty feet away, stood the man, a paper bag in one hand and a revolver in the other. In a split second, both men fired. Then the suspect turned and fled westbound for several steps, before kicking in the rear basement door to a rowhouse, entering, darting through, and exiting the front. There, officers who had arrived to back up the two partners leveled their weapons on the suspect, and he dropped down the front steps to the sidewalk.

Tabeling could not believe how quickly the thing had happened. He had reacted not because of any training but because of an instinct he hadn't known he possessed. There had simply been no other way to react. Charlie was at the scene by then. The ambulance arrived, and the wounded man was handcuffed to the gurney and conveyed to nearby Provident Hospital. He'd been shot in the groin, not necessarily a fatal wound, but once at the hospital, he fought staff efforts to help him. The exertion aggravated the wound, and he died on the gurney.

Back at the station, Tabeling's captain informed him that the suspect had died. The lieutenant inspected Tabeling's revolver, telling him that he would have to take his revolver from him. Three chambers of Steve's weapon held only casings; he had fired three shots without realizing it.

Tabeling then learned that he was to be charged with murder. Stunned to his core he was relieved of his badge and ID card before he could protest and then was taken before a judge to be formally charged. Bail was not discussed; he was released on department recognizance through a writ of habeas corpus. He was told to go home and to report to the captain each day at eleven until the matter went to trial.

He was horrified as to what this meant. Was he to be fired in disgrace for defending his life? His protest to the captain was in vain. In an hour, he had gone from new sergeant-to-be to accused murderer and was now informed that his department-imposed suspension from duty was without pay—and that a defense attorney would not be afforded him.

He had taken a life. As the enormity welled within him, his emotions intensified. Even in his ungovernable youth, the sanctity of life was part of his psyche. Despite numbing terror he had experienced during his youth, he had understood that every living thing was part of God's purpose. He had had no choice but to do as he had done. But he was sorry; he truly grieved that it had been necessary.

Years before, while he patrolled his Central District post, he had heard gunshots. He had sprinted toward the sound and had seen the shooter, obviously maddened by something, standing before a crowded restaurant and repeatedly firing his weapon.

He'd been fearful of firing at the man because of the risk of missing and hitting innocent diners inside, so Tabeling had launched himself across the street and had swung his hardwood nightstick in a powerful arc that descended sharply, striking the gunman on his neck and dropping him instantly, eliminating the threat. He'd risked being badly hurt to avoid endangering anyone, even the gunman. It was not a logical act. It was, he realized later, an *instinctive* one.

Now his home life was somehow dimmed by the enormity of what awaited him and the depressing realization that he might be sent to prison; that no money coming in meant he could not care for his family; and that his good name in the department, in the neighborhoods, and among their families was now tainted. Everything was different, darker by that moment's decision.

Honey heard him out and then tenderly held him. "You had no choice, Steve," she consoled him. "If you hadn't done what you did, you might not be here with us. Think of that. We'll get through this together."

Three weeks from the day of the shooting, he was ordered to appear before the Central District Homicide Court judge. Without benefit of a defender, Tabeling stood quietly before the bench, listening to a detective read the police report that fully described the incident.

The judge's expression reflected the gravity of the issue. When the detective completed reading the document, the judge pronounced his decision to the crowded courtroom.

"Officer, you were confronted with a very dangerous situation, one that transpired in a few seconds and that required the use of deadly force to protect yourself, other officers, and innocent citizens. You are to be commended for the courage and skill with which you managed this most dangerous incident. You are hereby *exonerated*."

Tabeling felt the air whoosh from his body, and his legs shook. Gratefully, he realized that the nightmare was over. He could breathe again. The next day, he entered the stationhouse to resume his duties.

"What are you doing here?" his lieutenant asked.

"As far as I know," Steve responded, "I think I still work here."

"Not anymore," the man replied. "You are a sergeant now. Yeah, you work in the Central." He extended his hand. "That's right. Best to you. And good luck, *Sergeant*."

CHAPTER

6

The fact that he had passed a difficult and demanding exam and made good on it was an achievement unique in his life. He determined that he would make good with this new opportunity as well. He belonged to a department that seemed to value him, his work habits, and his developing skills as an investigator.

Returning to Central District was a plus. He felt familiar with the place. Not that it was a plum assignment, far from it. Encompassing about three square miles in the heart of the city, it contained disparate neighborhoods—some quite affluent, others nearly destitute, and both often abutting each other along intangible boundaries. At the very center sat the energetic central business district, crowded with banks, department stores, and insurance offices, as well as multistoried masonry towers occupied by law firms, investment houses, real estate offices, and the like. The district ended on the south at the harbor. On Baltimore Street, just east of the business district, lay the notorious "block"—actually several blocks long and home to strip clubs, bars, burlesque theaters, and fast-food eateries. Prostitution on the block was winked at by the city fathers, even though City Hall, in all its ornate Victorian finery, loomed barely two blocks away, next to the courthouse. To the northwest lay the wide and always boisterous Pennsylvania Avenue, raucous at night as jazz echoed from the dance clubs out onto the street. It was an area fast becoming a mecca for drug addicts, triggering frequent shootings and other violence.

All the neighborhoods were graced with houses of worship, such as the Basilica of the Assumption, which lent its grandeur to Cathedral Street; although it had grown dowdy with the years, it still was impressive in its nineteenth-century charm. African Methodist congregations populated their churches, especially on the west side. A practical ecumenicalism prevailed: Roman Catholic, Baptist, Methodist, Greek Orthodox, and Presbyterian churches sat within sight of each other, representing every strata of the city and its people, lending grace and dignity, each to its own place.

Unlike the other eight police districts, Central was unique in its numbers. Its daytime population dwarfed nighttime residents as the center city overflowed with workers each weekday morning, and streets flooded with cars, trolleys, taxis, and trucks. There were exceptions—the block pulsed only after the sun set, when the clip joints and gin mills filled with visiting suckers asking to be skimmed by squads of painted and padded young things. Many women hailed from Pig Town or South Baltimore or West Virginia. The girls were adept at showing some skin and were good as well at the insincere arts: flattery and flirtation, convincing the yokels to buy them a drink *"No, silly, I want champagne. That's what starts my motor."* And the marks happily lightened their wallets for the tantalizing possibilities that subsisted only in their feverish imaginations.

The first few days found the new sergeant warming the booking desk chair in the lockup. The desk sergeant was responsible for booking prisoners and overseeing a crew of turnkeys and desk aides. Central booked more prisoners than any other district in the city, simply because it suffered more crime. A lot of the crime consisted of larcenies, from autos, department stores, cash registers, and occasional pickpocketing. Burglaries were common enough because there seemed to be much property to be thieved. TVs and record players were popular with the break-in crowd. They stole autos or occasionally a truck or taxi. In some neighborhoods, desperate thieves stole clothes off the clotheslines. Then there were far more serious crimes—armed robbery, rape, and murder.

Sergeant Tabeling's stay at the booking desk ended as soon as his commander realized what an asset Tabeling would be back out on the streets. Captain George Deuchler commanded Central with a blend of intellect, experience, and occasional wit. His was a tall, dignified presence. He was known to be energetic, approachable, and profane, as the situation warranted. Deuchler was a leader by instinct. He suffered no fools, spoke his mind no matter to whom, and stood above the crowd when it came time to do the right thing. That included looking out for his men.

"Steve, I want you to head up my plainclothes squad. Major crimes are what you'll concentrate on. You'll have four officers, all hard workers. Here's something you need to know. There's a grand jury looking into the block. I can't say if any officers are involved, but I want you to inspect each joint every shift. Is that clear? You keep me informed. In writing. Look at everything: liquor license, ownership, lewd dancing, prostitution—you know the drill. Let's not let them get over on us. Clear?" Then, before they parted, the captain added, "Keep an eye on the uniformed men as well."

Tabeling was elated at the thought of having his own squad and the whole district to work. He gratefully accepted, and the next day he reported in early evening. The plainclothes unit alternated day and night shifts. His first business was the strip clubs, but he knew there was going to be plenty of serious crime to occupy his attention. Little did he know …

The beauty of the plainclothes job was the freedom it gave to find out things—about suspects, property, guns, and occasionally a body. And at each stop of this crime carousel, information came their way. Everybody seemed to know about someone who was doing something he shouldn't. Information was more than power; it was access to solutions to complex, closely guarded secrets about who did what and when.

First, Tabeling was told that there was a "new" wrinkle in the central: kids on roller skates. One tossed an object at a lady's car stopped at a light; a second skated up to "assist"; the third smashed the passenger window and grabbed her purse, and then all skated off. This sounded strangely familiar to him, and after a little probing and discussion with the state's attorney, the mystery dispersed like fog in a breeze. It turned out that it was the same group of hoodlums from the Western District who were branching out. Once again, they were rounded up, arrested, and charged.

Later at trial, the defense attorney made a fatal mistake of asking Tabeling, on the stand, "Well Sergeant, how did you know who they were?" Unwittingly, the question was posed to undercut Tabeling's credibility. However, it opened the door that allowed opinions and investigative findings. The law is very clear on this issue. When you testify, hearsay testimony is not allowed, unless the defense asks the question, "how did you get the information?" That question opens the door for hearsay information.

But there were much worse things.

One afternoon a five-year-old girl, on her way home, stopped for traffic before crossing McMechen Street. A young man pulled up in a car and asked, "Do you live far?" When she nodded, he asked, "Would you like a ride home?" She got in.

He didn't take her home but drove many blocks past her neighborhood, past everything she knew. He pulled onto a small side street off Greenmount Avenue. There, he steered to the curb and pulled her little form toward him. She knew that she had made a terrible mistake. He had hold of her and warned her not to yell or cause trouble. Later, when he finished, he took her near the neighborhood where he'd found her and told her to get out. "Don't say nothing 'bout this," he snarled and then pulled away. She hurt so bad that she could hardly walk.

When Tabeling interviewed the little girl, he found her to be a very intelligent and mature child, who had a lucid and vivid recall of the incident and of the man. She described him in detail and bravely recounted all he had done to her. She remembered the vehicle; she had memorized its color and look as he pulled away that day.

And she recalled his license plate number.

Armed with this information, the investigators descended on the motor vehicle administration and in short time located the record of the suspect car and the man who owned it. He appeared ordinary, with nothing that really marked him as a beast who hurt children. An arrest warrant was obtained that day; it simply would not do to let this guy get a chance at another child.

That night good fortune smiled on them, when a conscientious Western District officer, Dick Nevin, found and arrested the suspect. Dick Nevin was older brother to Central District plainclothes officer Leander Nevin, called "Bunny" by all, who had notified his brother that there was arrest paper out on a guy who needed to be got. In no time, the man was installed in an interview room in Central.

Tabeling and Bunny entered the room and sat down. There was no table between the suspect and the police officers, only chairs facing each other. The suspect sat defiant, outraged that his freedom had been taken from him. Tabeling saw instantly in the man's eyes that this was not going to be an easy task.

"I am Sergeant Stephen Tabeling," he said. "This is Officer Nevin. We brought you here to ask you some questions. First, why don't you tell us something about yourself?" Tabeling sat directly across from the man, staring into his eyes. Just the three men seated close together. Uncomfortably close. It was stage-managed to give the suspect pause. He was here with these two burly cops, behind a closed door. They were the essence of soft-spoken courtesy, of course. It was all done to play tunes in his head without lifting a finger.

As it turned out, the man had been a professional baseball player, drafted by a National League team and assigned to one of its Minor League squads. He was comfortable talking about himself, but he volunteered nothing else that might be useful. His posture, however, revealed tension, like a spring.

"You know," Tabeling said, "sometimes we can find ourselves in a place we hadn't planned to be." The man frowned but listened intently. "I mean, it's the kind of situation that doesn't appear as maybe a bad thing, but later, when you look back on it, it is." He paused, searching for the right words to soothe the man. To get him to relax and let his guard down. To convince him that he wasn't the monster he was. That it could have happened to anyone. That it was, at worst, a misjudgment. Not the foulest of acts. That kidnapping, raping, and sodomizing a five-year-old was somehow something that everybody could understand. Like that.

It was challenging. Just being in the same room with the guy was hard, as it would be with any thug who could do such a thing to an innocent child. Deep down, Tabeling didn't want to soothe him or be considerate of him; he wanted to smash the man over the head with the typewriter. But he knew that doing so would profit them less than nothing. A broken head would get him free—and that definitely was not what was needed. This one needed jail.

He went on. "You know, things happen sometimes. Maybe especially between men and girls. I mean, women. There's a lot of feelings there, emotions that sometimes even we aren't aware of, you know?"

The man was buying none of it. He remained stiffly perched on his seat, glaring. After a time, he said, "I need to go to the bathroom."

It was well understood that failure to provide bathroom privileges to a suspect under interrogation might come back during trial, asking if this statement, *particularly an inculpatory one,* had been coerced. It was the same with failure to feed or give water. Granted, some officers were not above playing one or all of those cards, but Tabeling was not one of them. He approached from another angle.

"This is about a little girl who's been hurt," he said evenly, staring into the man's eyes as he spoke.

The suspect glared anew, but this time Steve thought he saw the faintest glimmer of fear, of recognition, as though he hadn't known. "I don't know anything 'bout no little girl!" he shouted. "Leave me out of here!"

They had been at it for hours. Though Tabeling felt little progress was being made, he sensed there had to be a way to get to him. Meantime, Tabeling decided to return him to the cell block. Get him fed and give him water. Even allow a brief visit from his mother, her eyes glistening at the trouble her boy might be in. All such privileges were recorded in writing.

Two hours later, they resumed. "I think it's about time we get down to it. You know, that little girl could be dead now. You ought to thank God she's not. Have you thought about that?" Tabeling leaned even closer to the man. They sat face-to-face, their knees nearly touching. "Tell me," Tabeling said coldly, "you got any children of your own?"

The suspect squirmed and then looked away, as though he wanted someplace to hide from this relentless cop. But Tabeling watched as wetness welled in the man's eyes.

Just as they got the suspect on the verge, there was a pounding on the door, first merely annoying and then growing in volume and force. It was a senior commander, demanding entry.

"This is the duty officer. Are you in there? Open up. That means now!"

The duty officer had entered the station and was informed they'd made an arrest of the little girl's attacker. It was a sensational story, and the local papers clamored for an exclusive. The duty officer was a man who knew how to primp his feathers with the media, and he was eager to do so.

Tabeling glanced at Nevin and shook his head. "Absolutely not," he said quietly and then continued the interrogation.

"Don't you hear me?" the commander bellowed.

After a short time, two notable things occurred, both good. The duty officer gave up and tromped away.

And the man, his gaze focused on his lap, began to realize that this was not going to go away. He said at last, "All right. It was me."

From my experience interrogating suspects, I have put several things into practice. The moral? Never go inside an interrogation room without knowing *everything* about the case. Let the suspect figure out you know more than he knows.

The second moral? Keep the suspect talking. Keep listening. The more he talks, the more he's going to give up. Lying trips up the brain. Having to juggle competing "facts" causes confusion and starts to make him stupid—or stupider. Go in knowing more than he suspects. Most important, do not give up.

And, if necessary, ignore the pounding on the door. Absolute focus, even if it takes twelve hours. No distractions.

Later that day, when Tabeling and Nevin had the paperwork completed and the suspect was on his way to city jail, Steve was ordered to the captain's office. Seated before Captain Deuchler was a red-faced man in a senior commander's uniform, who turned angrily as Steve entered.

"That him? Well, Captain, I'm telling you here and now that he needs to be thrown out of plainclothes. He ignored my order to open that door. This is insubordination, and I'm not standing for it."

Deuchler sat emotionless, letting the man vent his anger. "What are you suggesting?" he asked calmly as the commander took a breath.

"You need to throw him out of plainclothes is what I'm telling you! You need to get rid of this man!"

Deuchler looked concerned but maintained his impassive calm. Leaning forward slightly, he fixed his gaze on the commander's eyes and said evenly, "He goes, I go."

Hearing that unexpected and unwelcome announcement, the commander, red in the face, sprang to his feet and angrily departed.

Steve knew the commander only by reputation, but that alone convinced him this incident would not be soon forgotten. He was learning that there were commanders in the police department who cherished such clashes, quietly nourishing grievances for years, if that's what it took to finally exact revenge. A future police commissioner was to call it a "culture of vengeance," and it was a dirty little secret in the department.

So was factionalism: you were either a Mason or a member of the Knights of Columbus, the Catholic organization. Though both associations were laudable and existed to do good in the community, in the department they were oil and water—jealous and antagonistic rivals.

Police work, it seemed, could not be just the dedicated pursuit of bad guys. One always had to cover one's vital parts. And Tabeling realized that his captain, by defying the politically connected commander as he had done, had placed himself in the crosshairs.

CHAPTER

7

E ven with the arrest in such a high-profile case, there was no time to rest, regroup, or regenerate. There were too many people clamoring for admission to the Baltimore City Jail. They were practically breathless, awaiting their turns—at least that's the way it seemed to tired investigators back out on the street.

Holdups were a daily occurrence, as though the day would not be complete without reviewing the most recent armed robberies. Liquor stores were favorites; some of them had been held up so many times they invested in expensive bulletproof Plexiglass enclosures that protected from floor to ceiling. All business was conducted through a shielded turntable on which the patron dumped his cash or plastic and through which the bagged product was dispensed. It lacked the personal touch to be sure but gave the store owner a measure of security.

The months sped by and Tabeling, normally immersed in the fast pace of investigations, arrests, interrogations, and court prep and testimony, some days felt as though he was on a treadmill from which he oversaw victims, evidence, paperwork, and decisions. He prided himself on staying quietly focused on his part of the world: Central District and that familiarity brought some measure of contentment.

But larger issues were stirring. By the mid-sixties the police department was beset by one concern after another to the extent that high-level elected officials began demanding answers. It was during this time that Bernard Schmidt took his leave as police commissioner, and an interim commissioner, Major General George Gelston of the Maryland National Guard, stepped in. But the compelling questions—why were there so many vacancies? Did that necessitate that an officer work two or even three adjacent posts? Didn't that slow response time? Was morale as low as disgruntled commanders and veteran officers indicated?—went unanswered.

Finally, totally dissatisfied with the department's lack of answers, outside "experts" were brought in to do a 360-degree, in-depth examination of the department and find out exactly what was going on. The International Association of Chiefs of Police were selected, and they dispatched a team of consultants who descended on the unwitting department. Minutely examined were policies, training, discipline, report procedures (and the integrity thereof), medical leave, relief factors, and dozens of other more or less arcane issues of Baltimore police practices. The survey took many months to complete, and the picture that emerged was of a large, complex, and very troubled agency. Promotions often resulted from personal relationships, rather than test results and professional proficiency. Shopping at grocery stores via police discount was a common survival tactic for cops so poorly paid they could not make ends meet for their families—Want to get a raise? Resign and get rehired at a higher starting salary than you had been earning! Reports of serious crimes were filed in officers' hats in case questions arose. If no questions arose within a week, the document was *file-thirteened, which simply means throwing a report in the waste can without any action or officially filing a report.* The deeper they dug, the more issues emerged.

The lead consultant was a retired Marine Corps colonel named Donald D. Pomerleau, a no-nonsense skeptic who may well have viewed the assignment as a potential death knell to his budding consultant career. What he saw deeply troubled him. He concluded that what was happening in the sixth largest police department in the nation was the cumulative effects of years of mediocre leadership and unprofessional performance. Pomerleau came from a universally squared-away place. The USMC did not tolerate slap-dash procedure, policy, or performance.

Published in 1966, the International Association of Chiefs of Police summary, was a scathing denunciation of the Baltimore Police Department and its management, leadership, and officers. And its findings were to ripple forward through the decades.

Meanwhile, Sgt. Steve Tabeling was free to labor at his work, content that he had found a meaningful and challenging job for which he was well suited. One day he was investigating a jewelry store burglary in which watches, bracelets, and rings had been taken. The store owner was distraught; his inability to afford insurance made the loss graver.

Tabeling had developed numerous sources of information—pimps, bar owners, gamblers, businessmen, even newspaper boys. A tip came to him from a lowlife on the block that a certain horse-track denizen he knew had shown himself recently wearing a very expensive wristwatch. After identifying the man, Tabeling and Bunny intercepted him at the track and inquired as to the source of his timepiece. After the usual verbal chess match, he admitted he had bought it from a man. The watch matched the description in the burglary report.

Then a second tip came in that the watch seller hailed from Clarksville, West Virginia. Tabeling acquired enough information to get a search-and-seizure warrant, a skill he had developed years before while still an inexperienced officer.

He had come upon information that needed further investigation, the kind only a search-and-seizure warrant would supply. Approaching his sergeant, he asked for guidance and was told, "What on God's earth do you want to mess with that stuff for? Nobody here messes with that stuff! Leave it alone, Tabeling."

Undeterred, he continued to gather the evidence. Though writing was an ordeal for him, the narrative portion of the warrant affidavit required a precise format. It had to identify the investigator and specify his credentials—training and experience. It had to present the probable cause existing to establish that the crime under investigation was indeed a crime and had produced relevant evidence and contraband. It had to identify the premises or location requested to be searched and specify why the contraband or other evidentiary item or items were believed to be there. It also had to specify the source of the truthfulness of the information so as to inform the investigator that the evidence was in that specified locality, within that time frame. It had to be specific as to location of evidentiary items within the premises. In short, the warrants were not intended to be blank checks; they were intended to demonstrate that the laws about search and seizure, the Fourth Amendment's provisions, were being adhered to.

After much agonizing labor—starting, discarding his work, and starting again—Tabeling produced his document. Of course, it then had to be reviewed, approved, and signed by a judge. He had had few conversations with such august persons in his young career. So, if he was not totally confident in his product, at least he was determined to see it through, and he awaited the end of the day's court and asked to see the judge. He approached the serious, stern, robed figure, Judge Joseph Burns of the Criminal Court, and handed him the finished product.

After closely examining the affidavit, the judge looked at the young officer, and his expression reflected some admiration for the fledgling effort. "You've got all the elements in here, Officer," he said—to Tabeling's relief. "But you've got them all mixed up. Let me show you." And he proceeded to take the young officer in hand. By the time he was done, Tabeling, for the first time in his young life, felt confident about writing something really important. His new skill set was to prove an incredibly valuable asset in the years ahead. And, in those years, Judge Burns never missed an opportunity to tell the bailiff to bring the young officer back in chambers to critique that day's testimony and presentation. The learning experiences were priceless.

To pursue the jewelry store leads, Tabeling and (Bunny) Leander Nevin journeyed to West Virginia, where they got help from the state police, one of whom accompanied them to the farm in question. After a few heated words and the sight of the trooper's shotgun, they gained access, dug down in a likely place, got lucky, and found the stolen jewelry. It was a simple but satisfying case.

Back at work, they got a report that a woman had been abducted, driven into the county, brutally raped, sexually mutilated, and dumped. Incensed by the savagery of the crime, they gave the case highest priority. One of the men was described as extremely hairy with an Afro hairstyle, unusual for a white. No other leads showed up until one night not long after, when Bunny heard hysterical screams several blocks away and sped toward them. As he pulled up, he witnessed the assailant, who matched the description of the man, struggling to pull a woman into his car. Seeing the police, the assailant dropped her and sped off. But Bunny saw that the car was an Oldsmobile, and its driver was hairy like a bear.

The next day they used motor vehicle records to match the description and year of the car. They found one that looked good. They drove to the address listed on the vehicle record and saw the same vehicle parked in the driveway. Peering inside the car, both noticed an envelope on the back seat. It was addressed to the first victim. Dots connected, they arrested the man. He was convicted for the heinous assault and sent away for many years.

Cases appeared, developed, grew, and spawned other cases in a never-ending spiral. There didn't seem to be enough hours in the day, and the many long hours working often took Tabeling away from his family for far too long. One night he got a call from Honey that Sondra was terribly sick and begging him to come home right away. As he entered his home, he saw immediately that the child was having great difficulty breathing. She was highly agitated and nearly hysterical in her fear and pain. Steve scooped her up and raced to the nearest hospital, Union Memorial. There, a staff doctor attempted to comprehend her symptoms and directed a treatment. A second physician, Dr. Peggy Hansen, overheard the physician's orders and instantly overruled him—she had correctly recognized that the little girl was having a dangerous allergic reaction. She warned all that an embolism was a very real possibility and offered her services. Steve promptly opted for her care. Testing established that a combination of penicillin and aspirin had triggered the violent reaction. After treatment, Sondra's health was restored. Tabeling recognized how fortunate they had been. The doctor's precise diagnosis may well have saved his daughter's life. Dr. Hansen left the hospital shortly thereafter to pursue research in the syndrome that had nearly taken their child.

Police work could not be ignored for too long. This time it unwillingly drew him into the political realm several atmospheres above Tabeling's comfort zone. His growing reputation for stellar investigations and his integrity had recommended him to conduct a special investigation relative to corruption in the Baltimore City Police Department.

Tabeling was summoned to the Criminal Justice Commission office of Raphel Murday. Upon his arrival he was met by Mr. Raphel Murday, Interim Police Commissioner Gelston, State's Attorney, Charles Moylan and Captain Vincent Gavin. Mr. Moylan told Tabeling they had statements and firsthand information about an illegal lottery operation located in the 1500 block of Pennsylvania Avenue. Mr. Moylan showed Tabeling signed statements by witnesses involving a Baltimore Police Lieutenant and a Sergeant. Commissioner Gelston asked Tabeling if he had the proper investigators, could he handle this investigation. Tabeling's answer was he would do his best, but that he would prefer to pick the investigators. Commissioner Gelston said this would not be a problem.

Tabeling was told by Commissioner Gelston to report directly to him and State's Attorney Charles Moylan. Further he would have an office located outside of the police building. Commissioner Gelston said Tabeling would be given any equipment necessary to conduct this investigation. At the time of this meeting, Tabeling was a Sergeant in the Central District. Tabeling's new assignment would be listed at the personnel office.

Tabeling was summoned into the interim commissioner's office and saw Gelston's worries deeply etched on his face. The matter was a highly sensitive one. Tabeling was tasked with undertaking an investigation of police officers who had repeatedly been named as rogues for stealing drug money. They were known to frequent several Pennsylvania Avenue locations that were recognized to have criminal connections, including illegal numbers.

The street lottery—prolific, unlawful, and very profitable—had flourished in the city for generations, fueled by people's obsession with instant wealth. Habitual play gave hope to those whose lives otherwise held little promise, due to circumstance, illness, age, or lack of education. And it generated mountains of cash. Payoffs were made at 600 to 1; a quarter bet might net $150. Violence was rare. Even thugs usually steered clear of numbers runners. Knocking one off would lead to little but grief for them.

The issue had arisen when a witness, summoned before a crime commission, testified that she'd been entrusted with some sixteen thousand dollars that police officers had stolen from a numbers runner's car and cached with her. Later, detectives returned from the police, banged on her door, entered, found the money, and exited with it. That was the gist of it. There were two complications, both obvious: (1) the money belonged to numbers writers who had trusted the woman to keep it safe; and (2) the money had never been turned into the police department.

"Can you identify the officers?" she was asked.

"Why, yes, I do know their names," she said.

Both men were well known in the department. Both were prolific investigators who knew the west side well. And both frequented the 1500 block of Pennsylvania Avenue. Ergo, Gelston had been advised to get eyes on those premises very soon.

His problem was multidimensional. He was a military man, not a cop. And what seemed perfectly reasonable and doable to a soldier did not translate into the same for police. Men who knew the area in question scratched their heads on the surveillance issue. The most adroit of them understood that if even a molecule of police corruption existed, putting officers on it to ferret out bad cops demanded that cops of crystal-pure integrity needed to be found; then they needed to be entrusted with this bombshell intelligence. And they needed to be the essence of discretion and street smart and lucky.

They also needed to be willing to do what promised to be a thoroughly thankless job that might get ugly in a hurry. The principals named as the accused were anything but pansies. If they even suspected someone was watching them with the conceivable intent of putting them into a prison cell, things might get violent fast. There was that.

Then there was the fact that the interim commissioner simply did not know who he could trust. The commanders with whom he interacted seemed nice enough fellows, which proved nothing because most of them were quite adept at slinging bull.

The matter gave Tabeling a knot in his stomach. He had never contemplated investigating police officers, and he knew full well the scorn that cops reserved for a rat who might betray a brother officer. Doing such work likely could mark him forever. On the other hand, the mere fact that the acting commissioner had selected him from the department's many investigators was a source of pride, if an uncomfortable situation. The gears that propelled the department were sharp and could very easily grind him into paste. He didn't permit himself the freedom to refuse. When his services were requested, he made up his mind to do it.

He needed to overcome several logistical obstacles. For one, he could scarcely take his Central District squad into the neighboring district, where they had neither the knowledge nor sources they enjoyed in the Central. Besides, he didn't want his cops sullied by the detail; he wasn't sure they would have embraced the job of watching other cops. Gelston understood. Tabeling was directed to use the Western District plainclothes squad, but someone had to tell the Western District commander that his people were being preempted. Tabeling proceeded to the Western to do exactly that.

The commander was an old-fashioned cop who had come up through the ranks and was known by one and all on the west side.

As one of the few black commanders in the department, he was understandably possessive of his turf and prerogatives. As they made each other's acquaintance, the commander eyed Tabeling warily. Steve's explanation was short, to the point, and firmly nailed in place. "The interim commissioner Gelston has ordered me to do this," Tabeling stated matter-of-factly. "I really don't know what else to tell you, Captain."

The commander stood for a moment, letting the import filter in. "You tell me you are taking my plainclothes squad to work for a sergeant from Central District, and you can't tell me why? And to do some kind of I-don't-know-what investigation in my district, and you can't tell me why?" His demeanor, like the volume of his voice, was on boil and getting hotter. "And," he continued, his voice intensifying, "I'm supposed to just smile and let you waltz out of here with all that, just because some National Guard general is calling the shots?" He took a breath and then contemplated Tabeling, a look of incredulity on his face. "That's what you're telling me, Sergeant? Because that is totally messed up."

Steve heard the man out and then slightly shrugged his shoulders in an involuntary manner, not meant to be disrespectful but merely inevitable, as those were his orders. The commander considered his choices and bowed to what was inevitable.

That first hurdle was not yet completed. As Tabeling was introduced to his ad hoc special assignment, it occurred to him that he knew absolutely nothing about these officers. Regardless of the district of assignment, plainclothes officers were always hand-picked, interviewed, and their past records scrutinized. Their reputations were known commodities. To stroll into Western District and take over someone else's squad was a transgression. This extraordinary assignment gave him grave reservations at its outset, not to mention that at least one plainclothes officer troubled Tabeling. The man's past track record, his reputation, left Steve underwhelmed, first as to performance but more to veracity. Steve recalled that he had a tendency to embellish and to tailor the facts to suit his agenda. He was the kind that made excuses for why something that had been ordered to be done was not done. Like the street denizens, he usually had an elaborate story but seldom had the goods. Tabeling set the matter on "watch this one" and turned his attention to other critical concerns.

There was the question of equipment. Surveillance was tricky, especially in an area like the Avenue, which teemed with pedestrian and vehicle traffic nearly twenty hours a day. He needed a nondescript vehicle or a stationary location—though the latter very likely would give them away before they even got started. Maybe a truck? Or a van? And they needed cameras. *Special lenses*, he thought. *But from where?*

He stretched his memory and remembered a private company, a security firm, that might be willing to help them. Michael Meyers, a former army intelligence officer, ran a detective agency in the city and was approached for the needed transport and equipment. For a variety of reasons. Meyers was a friend of Captain Gavin and agreed to allow the unit to use his offices and equipment for this investigation.

Somewhat less than enthusiastic were the Western District officers detailed to the effort. Tabeling had known them from his time in the district, years before. Though most were trustworthy, it soon dawned on Steve that maybe Gelston had misgivings about several of the Western plainclothes officers as well and about their lieutenant, a man known more for boisterous and obnoxious behavior than performance.

The more Tabeling contemplated the assignment, the tighter the knot in his gut grew. But orders were given to be obeyed.

He gathered them at Memorial Stadium, a huge venue for confidential briefings but accessible, with loads of parking and, when unoccupied, very private. The briefing was necessarily opaque. It was to be a highly confidential matter and demanded discretion. Even other cops didn't need to know. The officers' countenances ranged from vague interest to outright hostility.

For the next several months the impromptu unit worked at surveilling five locations on the west side, alternating vehicles and shooting hundreds of feet of film of suspected individuals—a number of whom were police officers—entering and exiting the target locations. Each day a unit member parked the vehicle of the day at a different vantage spot and then locked and left the area, leaving an officer inside with the borrowed movie camera. One of the detectives assigned to the effort, Paul Karaskawicz, was an able photographer. The exposed 35 mm film was brought to the Fifth Regiment Armory each night for processing, scrutiny, and analysis. Within several months, based on the images and on a journal kept by the officers, together with subsequent interrogations, Tabeling had enough evidence.

He then filed and obtained a search-and-seizure warrant, specifying each of the five locations and linking them into a single criminal conspiracy—and thus one winnable case. Search-and-seizure and arrest warrants were obtained. Tabeling made copies for each of the arrest teams, to be used in a series of simultaneous raids. As rarely happens in such a complex, highly choreographed operation, all went off without a hitch. Ten gamblers were arrested. Much illicit numbers money was seized.

After the raids, the warrant and all copies were to be returned to Tabeling, and it was then that he discovered that the original warrant was missing. The officer who had been issued the original was *that* guy—"Officer Alibi." When asked where it was, he claimed that he had returned it to Sergeant Tabeling. The warrant had been stolen, and Tabeling immediately knew the culprit. This was the same officer about whom he had reservations from the start. The missing original was not a critical point. The trial could proceed without it. It was, however, an embarrassment, especially when the handpicked supervisor appeared unable to control his officers, particularly in so sensitive a matter.

When informed of the incident, State's Attorney Steve Moylan was confident the loss would pose no insurmountable issues at trial.

Nurturing misgivings nonetheless, Tabeling prepared for the courtroom. Once the reporting was completed and reviewed, all hands readied themselves for the trial. The defendants were to be tried in a single court case. After several contentious days, all were found guilty and sentenced, and Tabeling felt he had ably fulfilled Gelston's mandate.

Despite the fact that police officers, including supervisors, had been filmed entering and exiting the locations, no officers were charged—a decision of the State's Attorney's Office. Tabeling wanted to move on. After the guilty verdicts, he was informed that the department was starting a new intelligence unit and that he was to be its first sergeant and its newest member.

The year was 1966. The IACP report had raised temperatures all over the state of Maryland, especially since the Baltimore police commissioner was appointed by the governor, a provision designed to prevent the interference or control of the police executive by local elected officials in the running of the agency. It was then that Gelston announced that his time as interim police commissioner was at an end. When Gelston departed, Tabeling felt like he was sitting on a high limb of a tall tree. And that someone holding a saw was gazing up at him and smiling.

Donald D. Pomerleau was named as the new police commissioner. He'd come to town as a reform executive, determined to apply modern principles of management, assure a strong anti-corruption stance, and set new standards for police performance and professionalism. There was to be no more seat-of-the-pants decision making. Moving forward, the findings of the consultant study were the guiding lights. What followed was the most extensive overhaul, redesign, and reorganization of the Baltimore Police Department in its history. Nothing was left to slapdash procedures or chance. Kicking and screaming, the police department was dragged into the twentieth century.

But during the trial, the local newspaper, the *Sun*, did not concur with the efficacy with which the numbers men had been investigated and prosecuted. While the trial was still proceeding, the paper published a story regarding the missing original warrant and ascribed the incident to dishonest motives. The principals in the case had not been unduly concerned; trial progress had bolstered their confidence and reinforced their reputations.

Such equanimity did not prevail in the new police commissioner's office. Appointed with a clear mandate to square away the anarchic and, by reputation, corrupt organization, the new chief executive choked with rage at the article, which demeaned and discredited the department and, by implication, him, tainting his new administration. Tabeling and Captain Deuchler were summoned to his office.

A very anxious Peggy Krukowski, administrative assistant, bid them to enter.

Pomerleau was seated imperiously behind his large polished desk. Tabeling saw at once that that the chain-smoking executive was fuming. He gestured to a chair in the center of the room.

Without preamble, he snarled, "Explain to me, Sergeant, how you managed to take a simple assignment and mess it up this badly?" He threw open the newspaper article and tossed it aside. "This was an egregious example of very bad supervision. My first inclination is to fire you. I can't decide whether to fire you or demote you. But one thing is certain: you will never work plainclothes again. Not ever!"

Had this comprised the full extent of Tabeling's admonishment, the point would have been made as to the missing warrant in an unmistakable manner. But the diatribe and vilification still flooded like a tide. Tabeling, seated before the big desk like a school boy awaiting the principal, maintained his composure and sat silently. Behind him sat his captain. Both men had been chewed out before but never like this. This was a hall-of-fame reaming. In point of fact, Steve sensed that silence was the best course for both of them. They sat stoically and absorbed the new commissioner's wrath.

As he wound up his tirade, however, Pomerleau lowered his voice and stared coldly at Tabeling. "I'm not going to fire you. Apparently, you have friends in law enforcement. I leave it up to you. Pick a district, and that's where you're going."

Taken aback, Steve quickly collected his thoughts and responded, "Eastern. Eastern District, if that's okay."

The new commissioner nodded and emitted a grunt, dismissing them both.

When they left Pomerleau's office, two things were quite clear to both men: (1) Tabeling's career was about to take an unanticipated turn, and (2) Donald Pomerleau did not take kindly to anyone who appeared to sully his reputation.

Also, Tabeling was off on the obviously wrong foot with this new boss.

Years later, Tabeling learned that the warrant had indeed been stolen by the same officer to whom it had been entrusted. He had taken the document to a defense attorney involved in the trial, a bit of treachery done for cash. Ultimately confronted, he had denied any wrongdoing. He was allowed to resign.

Why Eastern? Tabeling knew it to be a tight bunch of officers who worked well together. It was not unlike Western and Central—problematic neighborhoods becoming inundated with drugs, heroin mostly, and robberies, guns, and violent crimes by the score. Fertile ground, in other words, for a cop who enjoyed the work. Plainclothes or uniform, it was all the same to him.

CHAPTER

8

R eporting to his new assignment, Tabeling was greeted by the captain, a plainspoken and congenial man known to all as a fair and reasonable commander. Tabeling was happy to be out of the toxic shadow of the headquarters building. The street suited him much better.

His new commander got to the point. "Steve, I need you to be the monitor sergeant for the whole district. Anything crops up, they need a hand, and you take it. And take care of the vehicles. Make sure everything's running smoothly—that kind of stuff. Okay?"

Tabeling was pleased. It was a responsible position that provided him with space and all the discretion that he could want. He saw immediately that the district was brimming with hardworking officers who were knowledgeable, experienced, and fulfilled by working cases and solving crimes. He met two men he knew by reputation, who were exceptional investigators, even by Eastern District standards. Leonard Santivasci was tall, olive-complexioned, and quiet. His partner, Robert Cohen, was shorter, highly intelligent, and, like his partner, highly motivated. They were totally compatible colleagues who had built an exceptional repute for exemplary investigations. They complemented each other and were a model team. They used lineup photos, numerous sources, developing more if needed, exhaustive records searches, encyclopedic memories of priors, modes of operation, weapons and injuries. They loved their work, and their work product showed it. But they were modest, even in their renown, and maybe that's what Tabeling admired most about them.

Inevitably they reached a case that stumped them. A series of armed holdups occurred, pulled off by a group proficient enough to commit jobs in daylight and vanish. The two investigators, recognizing Steve's past successes, welcomed a chance to get him involved. Reviewing the reports, the three of them formulated an approach to ensnare the crooks. Steve knew that information from witnesses and thoughtful planning were essential trails to apprehension. Witness description provided starting points; then it was in-depth looks at the suspects' habitual behavior, as it became apparent, favorite targets, and the like. All were productive beginnings. But Steve saw that these complex investigations needed to wield a specific approach. They lacked an overall strategy.

As so often happened, an informant tipped them to the identity of one of the suspects. They quickly felt out all there was to know. As always, knowing a man before sitting him down for a conversation always arrayed the dealt cards into a much stronger hand.

He was in his late teens, and this was not his first get-together with the police. Therefore, he might be wise in the ways of both the street and the police stationhouse.

Tabeling sought leverage with this suspect. Was he on probation or, better yet, parole? How did he come to know his criminal associates, the thugs he worked with? What health and habituations did he suffer? Where did he sleep? Where could they go to pick him up? And what time of the day was the best time of day or night to do that?

Not a student of good cop/bad cop tactics, Tabeling adhered to the demeanor that had worked well in the past: calm and measured behavior and answering questions when asked, unless, of course, the questions compromised the process of the investigation. Feed the suspect, give him water, and permit bathroom breaks. And always keep the suspect up to speed.

Tabeling said, "Have you noticed since we've been talking that I've been writing? I'm writing everything you tell me. It's all right here." He lowered his eyes to glance at it. "I've been writing everything you tell me." As he spoke, he studied the man's face for expression and reaction. "When we finish talking, I'm going to let you read everything taken down so you can satisfy yourself that those are the things we talked about. Nothing has been added or taken out, okay? I'm going to ask you to read each page and put your initials on it with today's date, if you're satisfied that what's there is what we talked about. That be okay? And if there's anything wrong with it, then you'll change it. All right?"

It was a highly effective device. Often the suspect's expression underwent transformation—from defiance, scorn or fear to a realization: "This cop asks me stuff, not just what I did but what I *think*."

Smoothly, subtly, Tabeling was admitting the suspect—at least in the suspect's head—*into* the process. He was not being made to feel like some homey being played; he was a person, somebody who had a say in this.

Once the suspect dropped his defenses, he might become more talkative, voluble even. It was this joining in his own life's decision that was something unnatural in his experience.

Tabeling proceeded. "But I've got to tell you, if you tell me something that you know isn't true, that's not going to be good. You know that, right? Because we want to find out what happened, and we can't do that with false statements." He went on to explain why cooperation was so much smarter than not. "Like, if you were to tell me that you did, like, ten holdups? That's a lot of time for each holdup, you see? But if you tell it straight, without any deception, then we can ask the state's attorney to ask the judge to set the sentences to run *concurrently*. Like, you serve one set of the years for all the crimes together, see?"

The man, who was following Tabeling's explanation with serious interest, nodded.

"But," Steve went on, "let's say you were to deceive us, and then we had to find out what happened from somebody else. You see that would not be in your best interests, don't you? Because when other people get involved, they might tell us things about you that even you didn't know. Or things that you kept from us. Like more things you might have done. Then we couldn't talk to the judge for you to get you concurrent sentences. Like, if you told us you did ten, and then we found out you'd done *fifteen,* then how could we go the state's attorney and ask for consideration for you? You see what I am saying?"

As Tabeling observed the man's features, he saw that the suspect was getting it. Just because he was a thug didn't mean that he was stupid.

In the end, best interests usually prevailed. People helped themselves. If there were two criminal partners in two rooms, once the scenarios were explained to them, there would be a race for each to turn the other guy inside out—to help himself.

There were exceptions. Some suspects were hostile and absolutely refused to utter a sound. They had that persona, and that's what they thought worked best. Or perhaps they *were* stupid and couldn't foresee outcomes. Some were sociopaths who believed they had an inherent right to take things at gunpoint—women, money, whatever they wanted. They had to be handled on a different plain; they had to be convinced they were dunking without a ball or riding a bike with no chain.

Over the months, Tabeling gained confidence and grew proficient from interrogating dozens of suspects. He knew, as all police know, that one cooperative criminal participant was good but more were much better. This was especially so in a criminal enterprise like the one facing them, where there had been over fifty holdups thus far. In each they had used handguns. These were serious felonies, dangerous as well. But the fact that no one had yet been hurt was a positive. *Maybe,* Tabeling thought, *we're dealing with people who don't rattle.*

Once they had accumulated suspect names, descriptions, hangouts, and the like, Tabeling, in his uniform, along with Santivasci and Cohen in plainclothes, piled into their plainclothes Chevy and headed off to those neighborhoods that might likely shelter the "thug of the month." They drove the narrow trash-lined streets, scanning stoops, storefronts, and alleyways, occasionally getting out of the car to show a Bureau of Identification photo of their suspects to a passerby or front-stoop nester. Nabbing one was a kick, no matter how many they'd grabbed. And each one had to be studied because each was unique. Whether stoic, arrogant, loud, profane, coldly furious, or some other variant, each was an enigma who held specific colored tiles to complete the mosaic of who he was and what he was about.

As each prisoner was brought in, Steve tried to read them. Bravado melted—or at least stilled itself—in a place where cops were constantly coming and going, where iron doors clanged shut, and where shackled prisoners were led into the station lockup for court and still others were shackled to return in the same jail van. The "what did I do?" expression lit on some of their faces almost immediately, even if most of them had been through the process many times. There were other expressions of bored resignation, or "Here I am again," or occasional impotent rage.

Few previous cases that Tabeling had dealt with had the numbers and complexity of this one. Worse yet, it was still progressing, as the gang continued with their robberies, even as their partners were picked up. Muddying the investigation even more was the fact that however many holdup men there were, the officers were fairly certain that each suspect had not participated in every robbery. From the investigators' standpoint, then, they had to build cases that could win in court and still pinpoint who did what, when, where, and how. That meant being able to prove that suspects A, D, and E robbed the grocery store at Ensor and Gay and got away with $107 on Tuesday, the twelfth, and suspects B, C, and E robbed the convenience store at Twenty-Second and Guilford two days later and got nineteen dollars.

What such complexity demanded was an overall picture of what they were dealing with. Once they nailed down who did what and where, they could proceed, delving deeper into the reports, the statements, evidence, confessions, and other evidence. Cross-indexing items that were common to two or more of the robberies and then going over them in light of the totality of the case shined beacons of light in the gloom of uncertainty. Adding corroboration cemented the foundation of any case—eyewitness testimony (at the scene and subsequently in a lineup), clothing worn, weapon displayed, orders shouted, and vehicles used (the make, model and color). All these and more bolstered each case. After some practice, they began to make inroads into the orchard of facts waiting to be harvested. After a time, it began to resemble an assembly line—mere routine.

Except they were dealing with dangerous criminals, men who carried powerful handguns and presumably knew how to use them, and like anyone facing fifteen or more years in prison, some of them might very well border on irrationality.

Lineups required planning, patience, and attention to the logistics of the thing. Usually the suspect was marched onto a lighted platform with five other likely-looking suspects—except they were usually police recruits, or passersby, or other civilians recruited for the novelty of the experience and five dollars. Witnesses stood behind a curtained viewing area and the "suspects," including the actual one, stared into a bank of lights, illuminating and blinding them at the same time.

When enough information about a location was amassed, Tabeling gathered all the pertinent facts and applied for a search warrant. Interspersed with regularly arresting suspects on the street, hitting houses usually netted fruits of the crime—articles of clothing worn during the holdup, sometimes even weapons. Depending on whose house it was, the police presence within the premises often supplied its own considerable leverage during subsequent chats with the accused. Search and seizure was a magnificent tool in the cop's arsenal; the trick was to master its investigative benefits, its language, and its use.

Tabeling had continued to study the law, reading the *Daily Record*, a Baltimore journal written for attorneys and judges, to glean new court decisions and their import. His legal knowledge enhanced his abilities as a cop and satisfied an old yearning for leaning—learning he could do for himself.

Despite a hectic work and court attendance schedule that consumed most of his waking hours, Steve determined to make time with his family. They all looked forward to the sports events the children participated in. One fall day, while the family stood on the sidelines at Kirk Field, young Steve, playing linebacker on his first sandlot team, was blocked by two players and failed to get back up after the whistle. Seeing the boy was injured, the game officials summoned medical assistance onto the field. An ambulance arrived, and he was taken to Union Memorial Hospital, where he was diagnosed with a broken femur—bad, though not bad enough to keep him down. Over the winter, he took to rehabilitation with a will and exercised to the fullest that he was able. By spring, he was the starting catcher on the Calvert Hall High School team. His worried parents were transformed into proud parents.

Meanwhile, the solemn procession of robbery suspects entering the Eastern cellblock continued. A lieutenant observed the perpetual parade of suspects through his district and accosted Tabeling, abruptly questioning his veracity. "That's a lot of people you're bringing through here, Tabeling. Do you know what you're doing? You giving them their rights and everything?"

Steve stared back quietly. "Yes," he said, "I know exactly what I'm doing."

He was summoned to see the police commissioner. No explanation accompanied the command. Puzzled at what he'd done wrong, he entered the waiting area at headquarters and barely seated himself before Peggy, the commissioner's refined and polished secretary, bid him enter. There, he stood at attention before the massive mahogany desk.

Pomerleau looked up and glared with red-rimmed eyes. "Captain Hasson wants you at Northern," he said at last. "He wants you to be his plainclothes sergeant."

Tabeling could not credit what he was hearing. He blurted, "I thought you said I would never work plainclothes again, Commissioner?" His remark was part candor, part smart-assed.

This elicited immediate and dramatic tenor in the executive's comportment. "You do what I tell you!" he bellowed. "Now get your ass up to Northern District!"

To which Tabeling responded, "Yes, sir."

The new appointment was a godsend. With his own squad of investigators, he could range freely, not just over the fourteen square miles of his district but wherever in the city the probes took him. The new assignment was part of a citywide effort to combat the drug epidemic engulfing the city.

He had fallen in with top-notch cops who were fully immersed in developing actionable intelligence about dealers, locations, and methods. Information was developed faster than it could be acted upon. Steve sat with the officers unfamiliar with warrant application preparation, walking them through the laborious process of preparing legally sufficient affidavits. In no time they were preparing search-and-seizure warrants for over twenty locations. The subsequent raids netted dozens of offenders, money, paraphernalia, and narcotics. More, it garnered front-page headlines in the local papers, one of which described the effort as the "largest ever."

Then high-priced furs were hijacked from homes, store, and furriers in the district and beyond. Investigators found a link between the crime and the crooks, and the thieves were arrested, and many of the coats and stoles recovered. The business community beamed with relief. Tabeling's crew was making a dent.

But the junkies kept coming back, like waves on a summer beach, and their suppliers were everywhere.

Late-evening workload was often driven by a phone call from a trusted source. "There's a guy selling heroin you need to know about. This guy is very slick, and he's working a real seller's market."

Steve Tabeling listened intently to the man. Heroin use and sales were engulfing the Baltimore market. Everybody wanted some. Addicts developed two-hundred-dollar-a-day habits within months of a first mainline injection. To feed the drug, the user had to steal and sell more than six times that value—every day. Any property that could be converted disappeared and was transformed into the drug within an hour.

Tabeling listened intently and scribbled; it sounded very straightforward. Identify the guy, find his supplier—that would take some time. And this was the tricky part—the source was not yet a trusted guy. He was new, and Tabeling took the information on a combination of faith, intuition, and instinct. The problem lay in the politics; the heroin retailer was a Baltimore cop. Worse, he worked a turnkey job—the guy in each of nine station houses who doles out food, medicine, and supplies to the hundreds of people locked in the cellblock every night and day. It really was a seller's market.

First, Steve Tabeling put two of his trustworthy Northern District plainclothesmen on a surveillance of the suspect dealer's supplier. It was a rowhouse in northeast Baltimore. Going out of one's district to do investigations was a short path to stepping on command toes. It was as close to sitting on the third rail of politics as a cop could get in Baltimore.

They sat in their fetid van for twenty hours until they saw their suspect enter the house, at a time and in a manner consistent with the informant's description—that fast and that prudently, finally corroborating that the story was real. They had their probable cause. Bingo.

The informant also told Tabeling that the dealer was getting his capsules from a pharmaceutical wholesaler on the east side. Tabeling grimaced; that meant getting the federal drug people involved, which always made things a little more challenging, but it couldn't be helped.

When the probable cause confirmed the reliability of their man, Tabeling and his officers drove to the heroin-dealing officer's place of employment, the Western Police District, the highest crime district in the city. Before they could move forward, their man's reliability was tested again. The informant was handed marked twenties to make a buy, and Tabeling's officer patted him down in the plainclothes police car parked across the street from the station house. He then entered the Western station house unchallenged. Several minutes later, the suspect officer exited the station, walked to his personal car in the parking lot, opened his trunk, and retrieved something— something of value, as it turned out. He returned to the district and his turnkey duties and for-profit venture. In the next minute, the informant reappeared, crossed Mount Street, and slid into the plainclothes car. He handed the suspect substance to Steve.

Entering the station from the sally port in the rear, Tabeling called for the shift lieutenant and informed him that he was about to arrest the on-duty turnkey. The shift commander listened attentively and then blanched as the import of it hit him. Tabeling had taken steps to soften the hammer about to fall. He had informed the area commander of the Western District, who had summoned the suspect lieutenant. The shift commander's first words to the drug-dealing officer were, "Officer, I want you to know I had nothing to do with this."

When he was told he was under arrest, the corpulent turnkey, known as "Porky," stood without emotion. He was taken in handcuffs to the booking desk in his own station house, charged, and driven to Baltimore City Jail. Porky's arrest put the amenities of the Western District lockup at one fewer: no room service for heroin users; strictly overnight accommodations.

Porky got eight years in the Maryland House of Correction, where a heart attack later did him.

PART II

INTRODUCTION

B y 1968, political, criminal, and social stresses in Baltimore had become intolerable. The heroin epidemic threatened to subsume and destroy entire neighborhoods. Overdose deaths were common. Street crimes, often committed in the need for drugs, ran rampant, and the city school system continued a downward spiral of poor performance, declining enrollment, and spotty attendance. Demands for police service accelerated, and the daytime and nighttime sounds of sirens were so common they went largely ignored, save for victims, police officers, and perpetrators. In a larger sense, 1968 only reflected the larger problems that lay dormant within the city: chronic poverty; substandard housing; rat-infested, garbage-strewn alleys; and crime and criminals awaiting their opportunity.

Middle-income families, both black and white, fled the city in ever increasing numbers, streaming into new or nearly new suburbs that sported good schools, porch fronts, lawns, trees, and parks—and no gunshots or sirens in the night. Tens of thousands of the departed did not bother to stay in Maryland at all but migrated farther north into southern Pennsylvania and sleepy localities like Shepherdstown and bigger towns like York. In those places, like the suburbs of Maryland, little crime occurred, property taxes were lower, and good schools and friendly neighbors sealed the deal. People whose families had been part of the Baltimore city culture and its life for generations fled and took their immediate generations with them. They left behind ground rent payments, the delinquency of which could result in the house being seized by court order; housing that cost more for blacks than whites; and property taxes grown oppressive. The government seemed utterly deaf to their concerns.

The riot that erupted in April 1968 grew out of the rage over the death of Dr. Martin Luther King Jr., but its embers had been smoldering for decades. The riot lasted for five fitful days, and by its end, it had claimed six dead and about seven hundred injured, many seriously. Five thousand people, mostly blacks, were arrested. Looters had wiped out entire commercial areas in nine neighborhoods, and over a thousand businesses went under, most never to resurface. It spawned food deserts—areas without access to local grocery stores or pharmacies. Dozens of neighborhoods were gutted. In response, the US Congress enacted the 1968 Civil Rights Act, which contained provisions for fair housing. Yet the emotional toll was far higher and was not pacified by legislation, no matter how well meaning. The 1968 Baltimore riots had set race relations back to the starting blocks and set the clock ticking for a future reckoning in April 2015.

In the book *Not in My Neighborhood*, author Antero Pietila wrote that the 1968 riots ushered Baltimore into a new political age. Facing a decade with a population two hundred thousand fewer than twenty years earlier, the city government began to wrestle with the vast problems these new realities brought. Besides a population of aging persons unable or unwilling to move, there were new generations of children born into impoverished circumstances; it was a population that needed far more public services than the generations that had preceded them. Tens of thousands of vacant homes were abandoned by owners who no longer were willing to deal with crime, with tenants who destroyed apartment interiors or skipped on rent, or with property taxes double any jurisdiction in the state and strict enforcement of building codes that drove repair and maintenance costs up. By the acre, abandoned houses degraded the city's appearance and image.

Left without even a modicum of maintenance to keep them standing, the houses decayed; some simply collapsed into columns of towering brick dust, usually with no warning. Emblematic of the neglect, political stupidity, indifference, and one-party rule, Baltimore became the poster child for ineptitude in government, at least until Detroit emerged to claim that position.

There were, however, two bright spots: the Baltimore Police Department and its sibling the Baltimore Fire Department. Both agencies still attracted top-notch recruits. A program to lure college graduates into the police department attracted hundreds, a phenomenon that never before had occurred; and the fire service entrance examinations were technically oriented and tough. In both services, physical standards remained high. These two highly professional agencies gave the beleaguered city a fighting chance in the decades to come.

The police department had a lot of help from their veterans, without whose accumulated expertise, things simply would not have gotten done. One experienced veteran was worth several new cops, but as the decades passed, the department began to lose its valued veterans. The reasons were as varied as morale, low pay, better opportunities elsewhere, or boneheaded policies. One commonality endured: the working conditions consistently declined. And cops do not become knowledgeable veterans overnight or without mentoring.

In the police department, the men and women with whom Steve Tabeling worked pulled their weight and more, trying to turn the ship around. Though the years ahead were to prove challenging, they were years of very meaningful professional and personal growth for Steve. He was fast becoming known as a no-nonsense cop and a first-rate investigator, no matter who was in his sights. His immediate future involved a move to narcotics, the downtown squads tasked with stemming the illicit drug trade flooding Baltimore.

CHAPTER

9

Many of the changes wrought by the new police commissioner were beneficial. Married to the professional standards espoused by the IACP, Pomerleau was determined to infuse professionalism into the Baltimore Police Department's bone marrow. A new field reporting system was created and installed, one that made it very difficult to "file thirteen"-taking a report and throwing it in the trash can-offense reports, in a far-ranging change that standardized reporting and made crime statistics reliable—and crime totals much higher. Failure to write and file reports triggered "stingers," administrative darts that pricked the negligent officer; too many could leave welts that damaged career tracks.

Payroll processes were modernized and streamlined. Though still cumbersome, they contained safeguards to ensure accuracy and completeness. General orders poured from the print shop in an avalanche of new and revised processes, policies, and procedures. Salary structures were modernized and enhanced. Uniforms were upgraded, and officer appearance vastly improved. Foot patrols were slowly replaced with motor vehicles linked to a central communications system by way of Motorola radios, allowing instantaneous contact and a much accelerated response to all crimes.

Recruiting incentives were instituted to help fill the depleted ranks. Recruiters visited military installations to harvest men returning from the Vietnam War.

Above all else, Pomerleau prized educational attainment. He believed that earning college degrees promoted professionalism and improved performance. All ranks were encouraged to enroll in college-level courses at any of the area's numerous quality colleges and universities. Hundreds of members availed themselves of the opportunities—the department reimbursed tuition costs. The new decade would witness unprecedented attendance and a massive improvement in the department's educational profile.

As the 1970s dawned, many challenges loomed large. It was to be a decade during which nearly a body a day dropped. The murder rate ranked Baltimore among the nation's top five most violent cities; the number of overdose deaths nearly equaled the murders.

Over all loomed the specter of drugs. Heroin use skyrocketed, and the army of addicts were numbered in the tens of thousands.

Tabeling's insecurity over his education never quit him. Months before, while still assigned to Central, he had overheard one of his officers talking about his "schoolwork." Curious, Steve had asked the officer and discovered the man was attending GED classes at the community college to earn his high school diploma.

The officer explained the concept. "It's hard, but you can make up all the classes you never had. Math, English, history, science—all of them. It takes a while, and you have to hit the books really hard. But I'm getting it down."

It was time, Tabeling reasoned, and within a week he had enrolled and immersed himself in the classwork that had proved his undoing as a child. He worked ten-hour days, hurried to the community college, and later sped home to spend some time with his family. He would be early out of bed the next morning to see the children off to school, bending at the waist to embrace his sweet little girls and his stalwart son. The added effort was a strain, but the more he exerted himself, the more he sensed the value of the return on his efforts and the knowledge it accrued him.

As always, his beloved Honey encouraged, prompted, motivated, and quizzed him. In nine arduous months, he was ready to take the comprehensive examinations—an enormous strain he had rarely experienced. On the day of the test, he was ready for the ordeal because of Honey. The all-day exams ended with him shaking his head. *Never* had he been so hard-pressed or felt so uncertain of an outcome. When the results were posted, he discovered he had passed every subject. He was a high school graduate! Even his parents were pleased, and he felt vast relief and quiet pride in his achievement.

Work did not relent. Besides narcotics investigations, his officers supplemented uniformed officers in extraordinary situations. A labor strike erupted and turned venomous at a soft-drink bottling plant, with picketers hurling rocks at company trucks. That was par for the course—until one zealot dispensed with the niceties and tossed Molotov cocktails. He eluded the police, who pursued him. A few days later, a man came forward with a partial license plate number. Motor vehicle records yielded the name and address of a former employee of the bottling plant. Once again, Tabeling used his search-warrant expertise. At the suspect's house they found bomb-making paraphernalia in his vehicle. An important and timely arrest ended the serious threat of more attacks and the possibility of loss of life.

When Steve had a few minutes to reflect, he took stock of the way in which the past few years had unfolded and how grateful he was that he had found work that was rewarding, if poorly paid. As he considered the future that lay ahead, he grasped an astonishing insight—he had not hated the school experience at all. He had lost the terror that once had sent him fleeing the classroom. Maybe that was because now the facts and figures made sense to him, not just because of common sense but because he saw that they had purpose. For the first time, he understood what the purpose was—that study and hard work bestowed their own rewards, dispersing the ignorance and fear that had demeaned him as a man and as a cop … and as a father.

There were, he decided, far worse things than night school. For the first time in his life, he realized that he could go to college, and he made up his mind to do just that. Before many weeks had passed, he had enrolled in a demanding undergraduate program— first at Baltimore City Community College for two years, where he earned an AA degree, and then, without pause, to Loyola College, where the tough academic program, run by Jesuits, cut no slack for students who worked full-time days and attended classes at night. Steve decided he would study psychology, the better to comprehend the multitude of personalities that peopled the underworld of his hometown and the better to understand things nearer to home.

Then, without warning or preamble, he again was contacted by Peggy, the commissioner's secretary. "Sergeant Tabeling?" she said. "The commissioner wants you at the Maryland House at 8:00 p.m. In uniform. Oh, and you are to bring Mrs. Tabeling along. Okay?"

Tabeling acknowledged her request and then stared at the phone as he returned it to its cradle. *What on earth did I do now?* he thought.

Honey was even more perplexed than he as she hurried to get herself presentable after a day spent caring for her home and children. Running late, they sped to the posh neighborhood that abutted Johns Hopkins University campus. As they entered the Maryland House, they were led into the banquet hall. It was filled with Kiwanis Club members, who rose and applauded. Peggy smiled and gestured them toward the front table, where she seated Steve and Honey as guests of honor next to Donald Pomerleau, who nodded to the flustered couple. The occasion was their annual Policeman of the Year banquet, and Tabeling was the honored recipient. To thunderous applause, he bowed and gratefully accepted their ovation with equal mixtures of euphoria and the familiar trepidation.

The commissioner rose to the rostrum. After thanking all for their solicitude, he was savvy enough to recognize that much good accrued to the department for recognition this intense. Steve could scarcely keep up with the commissioner's comments. Slowly, Tabeling absorbed the significance of it. This was *Donald D. Pomerleau,* offering thanks for this show of appreciation and community support for his man, Stephen Tabeling. Steve realized that little else that life held in store for him could ever jolt him like this.

He listened as the commissioner concluded his remarks: "And if ever you find yourself in difficulty," he said in a convincing tone, "you want to have a man like Steve Tabeling to call on." He leaned over the couple and patted Steve on the back as he said so, smiling warmly at the astounded couple.

Not much later, Captain Hasson informed Steve that he was being moved down town to the Criminal Investigation Division. The necessity for cracking down on the narcotics epidemic had never been greater, and the department was moving dozens of experienced narcotics cops into a centrally controlled operation with the capability to reach anywhere in the city and, if need be, beyond the city lines. Tabeling and his men were made detectives and applied their knowledge, skill, and talents to taking down the city's drug movers.

The primary need was to develop a network of informants who supplied timely intelligence concerning the movement of illicit packages throughout the city. Constant interchange of credible information was the hallmark of the operation. Nothing happened without accurate facts. Surveillance, mind-numbing but often productive, was part of the arsenal of investigation. Unconventional approaches were welcome as well. Little was overlooked. One night, acting on information about a dealer's vehicle, Tabeling shinnied to the top of a nearby tree and peered with binoculars at the suspect. Then he relayed the suspect's moves via radio to his crew on the ground.

Of course, politics played its ubiquitous role. One bust netted a top aide to the governor, which earned Tabeling yet another visit to the police commissioner's office after his lieutenant, who'd been briefed prior to the bust, failed to notify any commanders.

"Why don't you let your bosses know?" Pomerleau demanded. When told that notification had been made, he bored in from another angle, reproving him for his *political insensitivity*. Bottom line? The deed was done, could not be undone, and was out of Steve's hands.

It was an unpleasant interlude, but the work resumed again the next day and continued for fast-paced weeks. Steve and his officers redoubled their efforts to make illegal buys; seining illicit dealers into their contrived retail drug market and then landing them to confiscate their product and grill them for intelligence. They set themselves up in a hotel in Pimlico, luring a man who had jars containing thousands of methamphetamines to sell to them.

Steve was totally fixated on this and was mildly annoyed when the radio summoned him to call the station.

"Steve?" It was his lieutenant. "You've got to get down to headquarters this afternoon. The police commissioner is promoting you to lieutenant!"

Again, he could not quite gauge what he was hearing. He knew only that there was no way he was going to leave this location before the deal was concluded. "I can't do that," he responded. "We're going to have do it another time. I'm in the middle of a case. It's going to have to wait."

And wait it did, until the wannabe pill merchant was safe in a cellblock and charges were filed. The next morning, the police commissioner presented him and Honey with the certificate and the personnel order that advanced Steve to the rank of lieutenant.

The accumulated and combined experience of the detectives helped to peel away layers of the complex narcotics traffic into Baltimore. They learned that heroin was bought in New York at 114th Street and Lexington Avenue. It was 40 percent pure at that point, but it got diluted—"stepped on"—several times before it hit retail on the streets of Baltimore. Yet over time, the purity figure consistently ratcheted up. Dealers understood their market pressures; no junkie's hard stolen money wanted to buy watered-down product. Competition flourished, just like legitimate retail, over who had the best junk. The products got purer, which meant more dangerous. From the 40 percent purity of a few years earlier, by the time Sergeant Tabeling arrested the Western District turnkey, analysis of that eighteen-ounce batch showed 80 percent purity, potent enough to claim the occasional unwary addict's life. Overdose statistics reflected the new purity.

The immensity of the epidemic became more obvious as their work progressed. Each arrest produced information implicating another individual or gang; all of them worked to import the toxic product into the city. It wasn't a local issue. Narcotics was finding its way into the supposedly lily-white suburbs. The detectives encountered dealers still in high school. It was a plague that was not going to be swept from the city's doorstep without massive effort, resources, and drive.

Despite their promising early work, factional in-fighting resulted in the narcotics strike force being summarily disbanded. Then, for three weeks Tabeling found himself displaced, in limbo, working community relations as a superfluous lieutenant detailed to a district. During one such hiatus, he looked up from his work when a uniformed sergeant entered the room. The man scrutinized this spare lieutenant, studied Steve's nameplate closely, and said, "Say, are you that little kid from Wilcox Street who never wanted to go to school? Little Stevie?"

Tabeling recognized the man instantly. He was *Sergeant* Bill Lutz now—probably, Steve thought, because Bill was one conscientious man—the guy who got him to school and on time for a full year.

"I *am* that kid!" Steve stood, and they shook hands heartily; then both dissolved into gales of laughter. "Thanks for setting me straight all those months!" Steve said, and they laughed some more.

Tabeling had crossed paths with many cops who felt as he did about police work; they saw in Tabeling the dedication to duty it required to get the job done, especially when working complex investigations. Captain Jimmy Cadden was one such cop. He was a man of substance but nevertheless a modest man and a decisive leader. Cadden had earned the reputation as a first-rate commander. His command of the Homicide Division demanded no less; it was rightfully considered the most prestigious and most demanding detective assignment in the department.

Just as Tabeling was entertaining serious misgivings about his own superfluous assignment, he took a call from Cadden.

"Steve," the familiar voice said, "I have an opening down here for a lieutenant. I'd like you to come down and take the slot. Of course, the commissioner has to approve all moves to here. What do you think?"

Tabeling glanced down at the paperwork accumulating on his borrowed workspace and hardly had to think about it at all. As Cadden had said, it was up to Donald Pomerleau. Several weeks, later the word came from the commissioner's office: Tabeling's assignment was a go.

He would work murders.

His first brush with homicide investigation had occurred years before, as a Central District officer. An elderly man, working door-to-door collecting newspaper subscription fees, was jumped by a gang of juveniles who pummeled him to the ground and took the money. Regaining his feet, he managed to stagger into a grocery store, where he collapsed of a heart attack and died. When the medical examiner ruled it a natural death, Tabeling thought, *Well, maybe without the beating, he wouldn't have had the attack*. He approached the doctor and ran his theory by the man. The doctor agreed—no beating, no heart attack. The one thing had caused the other. The doctor offered his opinion that the man might otherwise have lived another ten years. Under Maryland law, any assault that resulted in the death of the victim, even unintended, was a felonious assault; therefore, it constituted at least manslaughter. With medical opinion under his belt, Tabeling approached the state's attorney for Central criminal court. After explaining the elements, he asked the state's attorney if he would prosecute such a case. The state's attorney said he would indeed, and the thugs were in custody forthwith.

There had been others. Steve was not an expert in the matter of murder investigation, but like any skilled cop, he understood some important features—that any information forthcoming had a short shelf life and that the first forty-eight hours or so were crucial to getting the story down right. Also, given a complex explanation for why a thing happened or the shorter version, the simpler version usually was what happened. Physical evidence was vital to a case but delicate; it disappeared in a crime scene that was not secured and thoroughly searched. It had to be legally admissible, or it was useless. Therefore, it had to be lawfully gotten.

Cadden walked Steve through the unit, introducing him to his detectives. Most were middle-aged men who nodded pleasantly and continued on with their work. Steve was struck by the weariness he saw reflected in their eyes. All routinely worked overtime each day; on top of which, there was court overtime, an exhausting obligation that often required men completing their midnight tour to shave, eat, and report to criminal court for a full day, waiting to be called to testify. Often the exhausted detectives got home, collapsed into bed, and were back at their desks a few hours later. Eighteen hour days were common.

The grueling, long hours resulted from too many murders and too few investigators to handle them. The unit contained twenty-eight detectives. They were charged with the investigations of more than three hundred murders a year—a ratio to resident population that was many times greater than any other big city in the country. In addition, all serious assaults, shootings, stabbings, vehicular manslaughters, any police-involved shooting, or any serious assault of a dignitary or elected official—anyone with some drag—all were the purview of the men in the Homicide Division.

It wasn't just the volume of work. It was the essential command to get it right. To clear the crime. To put the thing to rest with a clearance, either with an arrest or by exception and state's attorney's okay. To get into this unit was an ultimate—slackers need not apply—after first having apprenticeships as burglary detectives and then holdup. It took years of successes. By any measure, to be a homicide cop in a city splashed with blood like Baltimore was to have achieved penultimate cop status.

But assignment did not confer tenure. Tenure was earned through performance. If a homicide detective wanted to stay, he had to clear cases. Failure to clear cases was a guaranteed ticket back to burglary.

Steve Tabeling had no intention of going anywhere but here.

CHAPTER

10

It is a simple maxim of murder: the victims usually know their attackers. That certainly was the case in the early seventies, when analysts compiled reports listing friends, relatives, acquaintances, and paramours and found that more than 80 percent of the victims had known their attackers. The analyses seem oddly conceived to comfort the survivors, as if saying, "Yes, your son was murdered, but it was his friend Freddie who did it." As an investigative insight, it was and still is useful. Stranger-to-stranger murder, on the other hand, is a totally different subspecies of the crime, often making motives difficult to comprehend and thus confusing the search for the suspect of the investigation.

And like narcotics cases, homicide investigations succeed or fail on the basis of accurate information. Professional inquiries into violent death produce mountains of data, facts that need to be sifted, verified, prioritized, and recorded. An active investigation is a machine gathering facts, any one of which might discredit or alter the veracity of previously compiled beliefs or theories. Homicide cops need to have resilient brains. One new startling truth throws a week of work into the can, and then hypotheses must be painstakingly crafted anew. Inflexible thinkers are apt to suffer blinding head pains.

When twenty-six detectives and their sergeants are all pursuing leads, gathering facts, exploring relationships, discovering evidence, overseeing crime scene searches, and the other myriad duties that is their purview, the simple act of collecting, collating, recording, and safeguarding these mountains of data is a herculean task. Add to that the lieutenant's overseeing and supervising the activities of twelve investigators, noting progress, and allocating detectives as the winds of priority constantly buffet the unit, and the pace of the place flashes into focus. The effort is a nonstop talent show designed to winnow out all but the calmest and most deliberate hands and heads. Working while exhausted is encouraged, if not fostered. Drama is definitely not welcome.

Tabeling saw within a few days that there were serious flaws in the flow of the work and the administrative overview and indexing, without which the bundles of facts were no more than lawn clippings. A case folder included everything pertinent about that case. It was a totally invaluable tool, without which no progress could be gauged or next step directed. Some of the detectives, for totally human reasons, secreted the folders so as to maximize their time with them. It was the same mentality that might make an otherwise mature detective hide departmental car keys if he knew he had things to do and absolutely needed a vehicle in which to do them.

Even when they were available, Tabeling soon saw that up-to-the-minute progress summaries were often not entered. Each folder's first sheet was the synopsis that crystallized the current status as of that moment. He made it his practice to review each active folder, morning and night, and query the lead officer about the case status that instant. His scrutiny was unpopular; some thought it petty, particularly originating as it did from a man brand new to his rank and new to the detective world, as well as being possessed of zero bona fides when it came to murder investigations. They, on the other hand—each and every one of them—were seasoned veterans of the killing factory that was Baltimore. Who did he think he was? If they didn't know their jobs and demonstrate doing the jobs better than anybody else, they wouldn't be here.

It was a compelling thought but flawed. Steve had seen that the high-octane pace of the place encouraged sloppy processes and cut corners. It was a totally human condition, and he understood its causes. But in the largest sense, these men were the only humans capable of speaking for and gaining justice for those unfortunates who had been deprived of their ability to do so: the victims. Then, too, as with his examination of a synopsis after its author's departure for the day and the fact that it included sufficient probable cause to pick up the triple-murder suspect that night, rather than afford him the opportunity to kill number four, it meant allocating resources in a timely manner to possibly prevent another murder. The corrected detective did not take it well. It was one time when Tabeling thought they might come to blows. Time healed the rift, and in time the man came to see the inherent wisdom of his new lieutenant's concern.

Examining the folders was crucial. Keeping track of the various cases was as well; it was a demanding juggling act, as cases came in, got investigated, and were solved—or occasionally not—and new cases replaced them. Like a factory, the assembly line never slowed and often accelerated its pace during summers and the holidays. Information flowed through, continually altering in volume, content, interpretation, and stewardship as detectives got new assignments and laid aside those that were a week old. Priority cases and a deluge of shootings in which the victim survived all had to be cursorily examined. Phone call follow-ups and hospital visits had to be made; supplemental reports had to be completed. Worst was a victim who was shot in a prior month but expired in the current month; then there was a restless roundup of latest information. And always, the phones rang ceaselessly—state's attorneys, defense attorneys, the communications division, the morgue, the hospital staff, and victims' family members asking "Is there anything new? What have you found out? Is he gonna die? Is it safe to go home?" All of them sought a few seconds of reassurance, closure, or redemption.

Overworked detectives might be forgiven the occasional lapse of courtesy; most maintained an admirable level of civility, even when the requested information was well beyond their grasp because someone had the case folder out without telling anyone, as was prescribed procedure. Occasionally, a detective's temper flared, and an offense report or notepad might go hurtling across the office. But most times, good manners prevailed.

The new lieutenant soon saw that some method had to be devised to facilitate this vast flow of information. It had to be discernible and contain pertinent information: victim's name; place, date, and time of occurrence; method of assault; detective assigned; case folder number; and status—open or closed. Closed meant by arrest or exception. It was the mark of success. Success was color coded: a red ball for open, yellow for warrant obtained, and a black ball for closed. Lots of closed cases after his name reassured the assigned detective; open cases did the opposite.

Tabeling produced a board and it was massive; it had to accommodate all the pending cases, which easily could be upward of fifty. He crafted the lettering so that it was easily legible from anywhere in the squad room. That way, anyone on a phone call could easily look up and see the status of the case in question. And, for the first time, Tabeling had a visual device that helped him to focus on the true big picture. It helped him with assignments, when, for example, one detective got bogged down and needed a hand or if another just needed an assist. At a glance, the stars of the shift shone brightly; the less productive showed themselves as well. The board instantly, silently, resounded as the exquisite management tool it was intended to be.

Not surprisingly, it didn't sit well with the detectives, most of whom viewed the status display as an unwarranted intrusion into their domain. The introduction of a clumsy management device, they thought, was to inspire competition among them or, worse, compare the quality and measure of their work, an unthinkable concept in police world. Grousing increased. But over time, as the utility of the board was tested, the detectives came to use and depend on it, and the board was grudgingly accepted, sparking the occasional ribald commentary regarding a member's successes or lack thereof. In time, the board evolved into a formidable feature of the homicide unit. As a testament to its functionality, it is in use to the present day.

Of course, the pace of murders did not slow to allow time for pressing management and administrative chores. One day Tabeling got a call from a trusted colleague who worked homicides in Baltimore County, and he had something for Tabeling that was rather removed from the normal city killing.

"We turned up a body on the shoulder of Route 40," he told Steve. "He was wrapped up tight in a blanket. Tossed there, I guess, like from a car or truck. I'm getting the morgue wagon to deliver him downtown if you want to get a look."

Tabeling and a single detective met the county detective at a Preston Street apartment house. There, identification of the blanket was confirmed by the apartment owner. He had supplied the blanket to the apartment and it was a very unusual blanket. The deceased was a heavy who did occasional muscle jobs for local hoodlums. Later, they took the blanket to the man's Preston Street apartment, where it was identified as belonging to the building, the same address as in the man's wallet. He was a local. Investigation took weeks and gradually revealed a convoluted scheme that involved a work stoppage ordered by a union leader at the site of a local hospital. The stoppage was intended to demonstrate influence and to jack up hourly wages for all.

It probably would have gone as intended but for a stand-up foreman named Klauss, who refused to allow it. He ordered his bricklayers to keep at work. After weeks of sifting evidence and locating witnesses, Tabeling learned that the foreman's obstinacy had infuriated the labor leader. Determined not to be defied, Phil Fiorino, the suspect in the killing of Hatfield, in turn, contacted one of his back-breakers to get somebody to straighten the man out—not kill him, just mess him up. Enter the late Mr. Larry Noble, who, in his eagerness to please the big boss, hijacked the man and carried him to an apartment to continue the session in privacy.

But something went seriously wrong there, and Mr. Klauss's life was taken from him. When informed of this blunder, the boss man went apoplectic. Hardly able to control his temper even in moderate times, he ordered his man to kill the offending underling who had made such a mess of things. On the day in question, Mr. Noble answered the doorbell to his Preston Street apartment to face a man with a gun, who shot him dead in the doorway, dragged the corpse inside, snatched a blanket from within, and wrapped the dead man tightly inside. It was probably a straight shot out Franklin Street to Route 40 West.

As the investigation proceeded, more and more unanticipated factors flashed on the radar. This particular boss left a trail of broken limbs—and occasionally skulls—as he exerted his will on workers at various job sites. Tabeling kept hearing recurring names. Foremost, he heard the same name: Eddie Murphy, a local who had grown up in a good family, graduated from parochial high school, and then decided to embark on a seaman's career. He procured a job with a shipping company and set sail. After a time, working on the ocean-going vessel must have revealed itself to be the drudgery it was, and he returned home to Baltimore. He gravitated to working with his hands and attracted this particular boss' attention. By the time of the killing under scrutiny, he was something of a go-to guy for his boss—as a breaker, though, not a fixer.

Beyond the complexity of the case, progress might have been smoother had the police department embraced the fact that it was a Baltimore homicide. But jurisdictional disputes over who got killed where were as old as police work. Nobody wanted an extra body, and Tabeling's captain was forthright in trying to extricate his harried detectives from pursuing promising leads.

Eventually there was sufficient probable cause to pick up Murphy. He didn't come quietly. Despite being charged with the murder, he had sufficient local clout to make bail, and he made no secret of the fact that he held Steve Tabeling personally responsible for this humiliation. Leaving the courtroom, he spied Tabeling across the crowded antechamber.

"Tabeling, you son-of-a-bitch!" he shrieked. "I'm going to kill you!"

Steve had learned enough about the man's vicious past to weigh the threat very seriously, especially so for his family. Honey took the news calmly, though a new worry line etched itself above her eyes. He reassured her as well as he could.

"The captain knows about this," he told her. "He's going to make sure we have police officers here around the clock."

Undeterred, Murphy contracted a women, convincing her to pose as an informant to the police. He instructed her to call Tabeling and tell him she had information on a murder. "Get him to meet you," Murphy said, "at the bar you frequent."

The woman knew enough about Murphy to fear for her safety, but she wanted no part of luring a cop to his death. On the afternoon of the meeting, she telephoned the homicide office and told the answering detective to warn Lieutenant Tabeling that the suggested meeting was an ambush. Murphy was again arrested, though this time he was to remain inside, awaiting trial. His attorney argued for a change of venue, and the judge allowed it.

The police presence around Tabeling's home worked on everyone's nerves, including the children's. More disturbing was that the police commander with whom Tabeling had had a run-in years earlier expressed to the local press that perhaps Lieutenant Tabeling suffered from an "overactive imagination" and that police resources detailed to secure his private residence were a superfluous expense. Incensed by the slander, Tabeling opted to end the security detail, requesting a shotgun instead. He slept with it beside him for several months.

The trial of defendant Murphy convened in Centreville on Maryland's eastern shore amid much scrutiny. Rarely did a big-city murder trial occur in picturesque Centreville. The state's attorney's case melted when a vital witness pled the Fifth Amendment. Ably assisted by a first-rate defense attorney and a forensic psychiatrist, Murphy was able to establish that he was not competent to stand trial by reason of insanity. The proceedings determined that he was a paranoid schizophrenic, and he was committed to a state mental hospital. Assertive legal representation later secured his release, and, to Tabeling's enormous relief, he relocated to Arizona. Though he had lost the case, Tabeling took great comfort in the fact that Murphy was no longer a threat to the Tabeling family.

In the day-to-day management of his shift, Tabeling realized that sometimes a boss needed to discern eddies in the current. The case of a renowned politician shotgunned to death and discovered in the garage of his affluent residence was prominent among such. Street talk had it that he had been deeply involved in the very narcotics trade his rhetoric often denounced. Even more interesting were the rumors that fed the gossip—that he'd been done in by a vigilante-like movement operating way outside of the law, ostensibly to curtail the very real menace the drug epidemic posed in the neighborhoods.

The killings did not stop with the murder of the official. More occurred; infamous narcotics peddlers were gunned down, not by rivals but by citizen do-gooders with guns. The trend was already quite troubling on a number of levels, not least of which was that a counterculture spawning another wave of killings in a city awash in blood did not bode well. To be sure, none of the victims was widely mourned. Information was spotty. Yet even people who despised the police recognized the threat such violence posed. As Tabeling's detectives gleaned nuggets of insight about the shooters, amorphous images coalesced into probable identities.

The police commissioner took the long view. Projecting the logical direction forward of such doings from his vantage point led him to conclude nothing remotely good for his city or his department. The specter of people enacting retribution suggested anarchy.

Tabeling had monitored the cases as each unfolded, discerning that these killings were far different than the nearly daily fatal shootings. The murders were more akin to political assassination—people were being murdered for their illicit trafficking. It was understandable, to be sure, but deeply troubling. In close daily consultations with his investigators, Tabeling had gathered fragments of information and insights until patterns developed. And though many of the conclusions he drew were speculative, identities emerged of five men. Perhaps they were motivated by a sense of outrage because so many black youths had succumbed to violent deaths, addiction, and the need to commit violent street crimes to support their habits. Were they doing the city a favor?

He had a good idea of their identities. Summoned once again to the big office, he was asked by a concerned Donald Pomerleau to offer solutions.

"We've been looking at this around the clock," Tabeling said. "Problem is, they're very clever. They plan and execute these killings with care. In and gone. No witnesses—at least none good enough to testify. Or willing to, for that matter."

"So what's the solution, Lieutenant? Do you mean to say we just wait for them to make a mistake? How many more deaths does that entail?"

It then occurred to Steve the man had called for him, despite their bumpy past. *Why?* he thought. *Could it be that Pomerleau trusts my judgment?*

"Well," Steve said at last, "sometimes you have to be creative. Not working outside of the law; that's not what I'm suggesting. But maybe get in their sight picture. By that I mean that not all surveillances need to be totally covert. If I was contemplating committing a crime, but I knew the police were on my every move, I think that would convince me to maybe not ... you see? Show them we *know*; show them we care, in other words."

The commissioner stared absently above Tabeling's forehead, as though contemplating the concept and whether or not it would bring embarrassment to the department. Just as vital, would it work? Would it stop them from killing anyone else?

"It's not going to be an easy or a quick fix, Commissioner. And with our workload, we're going to be stretched. But ..."—his voice trailed for an instant—"I think it's worth a try."

Pomerleau thought about it, and he dismissed Tabeling with a wave of his hand.

Steve knew one thing: the detectives tasked to keep an eye on the shooters were already less than enthralled with their extra duties. "Let them see you," Tabeling directed them, which triggered more grumbling. But they continued their daily—and nightly—dogging of the suspects; clumsily, as instructed, feeling unprofessional. It was an affront to their amassed abilities, yet they complied, making certain they were *seen*—not just rarely but often. It made sense that a man contemplating taking another man's life must truly reflect on it—did he really want to spend twenty-five to life in the Maryland House of Correction? Based on the surveillance methods, the murders ceased. Unconventional tactics had worked.

With Steve's new obligations, he realizes how removed the management role was. It demanded that he look at things with totally different eyes. He could hardly credit the changes overtaking him. The pace was blinding. Besides assisting in multiple cases, he coached the detectives. Some still were not adept in writing search warrants. Because warrants were vital to their job, he sat with them while quietly demonstrating the law, his insights, and the language devices that greased the wheels of the complex process. When he could, he addressed roll call training. Some still had problems with the Miranda rights—when to give them, when they were simply not necessary.

The detectives grumbled more. "Where are the victims' rights?" they asked.

"Never mind," Steve told them. "Doing it lawfully makes you better at what you do; it makes you do it better. When in doubt, get a warrant." He'd been coached by judges and state's attorneys. All assured him that the warrant nailed the case shut—and searches conducted without warrants were asking to have evidence excluded. Cases like that were lost because of laziness.

To ensure he kept up with case law, Steve subscribed to a monthly law service. It was expensive—really more than he wanted to shell out—but it kept him cutting-edge. Occasionally he was able to explain new developments in courtroom evidentiary rules to the attorneys. He was developing a fixation with learning and acquiring knowledge that he could put to work.

Always, he pushed the detectives. There was precious time in the unit for anything other than working nonstop. He wasn't one to pat them on the back for doing their jobs well because that was what they were *supposed to do.* They were the best; that's why they were here. Although he wasn't effusive with praise, he took quiet pride in being part of them and of commanding them.

When not immersed in the coordination of the murder detectives in a city besieged by homicides, he was in school—three, sometimes four nights a week. There was homework and papers, but writing still stymied him. Syntax, narrative expression, topic sentences, grammar, continuity of thought, and theme development all bedeviled him. As always, Honey was there for him, no matter that she'd be exhausted from her day. Each night when they reunited, it was if the years melted away and, with the children fast asleep, like a fresh start together again. It was exhausting, but now the compulsion to continue and to finish engulfed him, and he waded through the fatigue and plodded on.

It was the nature of the work that it never let up. The nude body of a young women was discovered tossed on the street in east Baltimore, dead of blunt-force trauma, her clothes thrown on to an adjacent rooftop. Detectives canvassed neighbors and pieced together the fundamentals: she was Gloria Burns, age twenty-five, and she lived down the street. Last seen yesterday afternoon. No family to speak of, but she had a boyfriend, Don Wilcox. He was around the neighborhood four or five nights a week and stayed with her in her rooms, usually. He hung out in a gym and worked out a lot. "Probably there now," most said. "He's a boxer."

They developed information and got an arrest warrant, and a uniformed officer picked him up at the bus station. The victim might as well have been an orphan; no one had come forward to claim the body. Tabeling took an interest and studied the boyfriend as he was brought in to one of the interview rooms. He was of medium build, dark-complexioned, and obviously fit. He appeared neither perplexed nor anxious and radiated a silent insolence.

Tabeling entered the small room and sat before him. "I'm Detective Lieutenant Steve Tabeling," he said calmly. "I need to ask you some things. Let me advise you of your rights. You have the right to an attorney ..." After he'd finished, he said, "Now, this is about Ms. Burns. Okay?"

Wilcox averted his eyes but nodded. "Yeah," he said. "But I want my lawyer here when you do this."

"Okay" said Steve. "Who's your attorney?"

"I don't know his name. I mean, my mother has his name. Can I maybe call and get the information?"

Tabeling knew enough not to interrogate someone who had asked for a lawyer. He got the information and let the man place his call. The lawyer was contacted but never showed. After the wait for the attorney, Wilcox finally relented, as if there was something he needed to express.

Steve began. "I'm curious. Just how long did you know Ms. Burns? Were you steady together?"

Wilcox swiveled in his chair. "We ... I mean, her and me ... we were going out for a time. Wasn't anything real serious. Not really."

Tabeling stared at the man, noticing his marred cheekbones and creased nose. "You weren't close, then? How was that? Didn't you ever stay the night with her?"

Wilcox scowled. "No, man, it wasn't like that. We did drinks sometimes. Ate together, you know."

"Did she cook?" Steve asked. "Did you eat at her place?"

The man shook his head. "Not much," he responded. "Once in a while is all."

"I need you to help me out here," Steve said. "We got neighbors said you stayed there four, five nights a week. Most of the week, in other words. Is that true?"

"Yeah. Some weeks, maybe."

"Okay, then. So what kind of friends were you?"

"You know," said Wilcox. "Sleep friends. I really didn't know her that much until the last few weeks, a month or so. She was getting … I don't know, clingy. Like women get."

"Okay," Tabeling replied. "So what happened then? She got on your nerves sometimes?"

"Sometimes. I guess so, you know, man? Like sometimes I just wanted to be let alone. Sometimes I just needed some quiet, going from work, to the gym, to the fights. You just want peace."

"And Ms. Burns wouldn't let you be? That it?'

"It's not as if I touched her. When they told me she was found like that, I couldn't believe it, you unnerstan'? Like somebody beat her and hurt her bad. Like she was assaulted; you see what I'm sayin'?"

"What makes you think that?" Tabeling asked.

"Her clothes. She was naked. Who? What kind of man would do that?"

Tabeling merely stared at the man, noticing that his defiance was crumbling.

"I know my strength, Officer," he said at last. "I'm not the kind that beats on women. No, sir. That's not me." He returned the gaze, but his expression wavered after a minute. He looked to the side, away from Tabeling's stare.

"So," Steve finally said, "you think she was sexually assaulted because her clothes were gone? Did you know how she died?"

The man shrugged. "Looked to me like somebody hit her real hard. Like a punch to the jaw." The man stared back for an instant.

"What kind of punch could kill somebody like that, Mr. Wilcox?" Tabeling asked. "I mean, is that even possible to kill somebody with a single punch? Help me out here." He paused for a few minutes before continuing. "I'll tell you what I think. Could it be somebody was trying to make it look like something that it wasn't? What do you think?"

Wilcox looked stricken.

Tabeling continued. "I mean, it's an innocent girl, right? Who could do such a thing and leave her like that?" He stared at the man. "Do you have any ideas? Did that happen for somebody to cover his tracks? Make it look like somebody else did this? I've got to ask you. Did you ever lose your temper? Did you ever punch her? In the face? Help me understand how this could happen."

Wilcox rubbed his eyes with both hands, massaging them as if to make this relent. Then he leaned forward, forehead in hand. "You gotta understand," he said finally. "It was never my meaning to hurt her. But she wouldn't stop! I just wanted peace, that's all."

"So you hit her? Then you saw she was hurt bad? More than you thought? Then, what?"

"Oh, man." Wilcox exhaled heavily. "Then I guess I panicked. I guess I thought if they found her like that, everybody'd think somebody real bad had done that. I panicked. I didn't know what to do. I didn't mean to hurt her; I swear. I just lost my temper for a minute, is all."

Tabeling asked the case detective to finish the folder and the reports.

Every day was an education, and today he had learned that asking for the suspect's help sometimes worked.

Kikoros was a contract killer who joined into an alliance with a woman who wanted her sailor husband deep-sixed. With the deed done, the two motored off to a downtown hotel, where a tip to Tabeling was enough to draw the lieutenant, with a trusted sergeant, Ron LaMartina, at his side.

Locating the room, they listened at the door. Hearing nothing, they put their collective free shoulders to it on a three-count, and it collapsed into splinters. There, supine on the bed, not ten feet from them, lay the suspect and the new widow, sans her mourning dress. Beside the man was a sawed-off shotgun, and he reached for it as the significance of the moment dawned on him. Tabeling and La Martina launched themselves in a shallow arc that culminated on the suspect, and he surrendered without further incident. On top of a hefty sentence for the murder conviction, the judge gave him fifteen additional years for the illegal shotgun.

CHAPTER

11

T he school year neared completion; Steve was finishing up his second-to-last semester at the community college, majoring in political science. Planning his academic career, he considered area colleges and universities. Several of his colleagues in the police department attended or were graduates of Loyola, a prestigious and demanding institution run by the Jesuit Order. The priest counselor informed him of which classes to complete at the community college before entering Loyola. In 1969 he received his associate of arts degree, his first, and he was eager to continue his college career.

Still, death shadowed the periphery of his life, as befits a murder cop. Most of the crimes his men investigated contained at least an atom of sense or reason, enough of either to make the investigator understand that though the act was reprehensible, the crime had a *rational basis*. Understanding the rationality of the act often played a role in the solution. There was something reassuring in it, as though humans had not reverted to a passing stage of savagery for no reason.

Random murders were rare but a flare-up of one could leave a veteran investigator with a migraine. Thrill killings had no discernible trigger, logic, or perceptible end. So it was that when bodies began to appear in south Baltimore, investigators were hard-put to determine motive. Suspects seemed elusive, as well as witnesses. Someone (or someones) were shooting and killing people, none of whom had anything in common other than their shared misfortune to have been in a wrong place at a wrong time and that they were homeless and helpless.

For days investigators trudged the length of Hanover Street, knocking on doors, with little or nothing to show for the effort. Then one day a tip came in that led the detectives to believe a gang of juveniles might be involved. By then, there were four dead and one person seriously injured. Canvassing again to identify gangs of youths, the detectives were steered to one particular group that was local, threatening, and frequented the area.

As the boys were rounded up, each was interviewed, one at a time, and each refused to talk. One boy sat defiantly and refused to utter a sound but was eventually convinced by his father. "Tell the policeman what he needs to know, Gerard," the man said sternly. "Go on; you tell him."

The boy reconsidered and turned to Tabeling. "We had some guns, and I guess we each wanted to see who the best shot was. First we tried cans and bottles. And that was okay, but we got bored. So then we shot at birds. But they're hard to hit. Then one of the guys shot at a car driving by. So then we all tried that. Then somebody said, 'Why don't we try a person? Like a real person and see who can do that?' So we did."

The investigators let out a collective sigh of relief. And the killings stopped.

With barely time to absorb that and continue on, Tabeling now fully comprehended the import of his position, even as he continued to grow into it. The detectives had gotten the message by now that their lieutenant, though strict, was fair and expected every one of them to pull his own weight every minute. There was no other way. Because some days it seemed that the crime of murder was specifically devised for the city of Baltimore. The killings came in every ghastly, disturbing form one could imagine. And solving one in no way curtailed the stream of murders backed up behind the most recent, all in line and waiting to be committed. Anything else was too much to contemplate, so Steve focused his attention on the current *crisis du jour* at the current moment.

But there was more. Occasionally the police commissioner tasked him not merely with solving a homicide case but also in thoroughly investigating it and determining if there was police officer wrongdoing involved. Internal investigation duties were sent to him for reasons he could not fathom. But lieutenants don't get a vote on such matters. So he did them.

One officer, proceeding in uniform but off-duty, was focused on getting home and relaxing when a car cut him off and nearly caused him to swerve out of his lane. Startled, he leaned on his horn and accelerated to pull closer to the offender and express his outrage. As he pulled abreast, he saw the other driver, wild-eyed with rage, gesturing back to him. Then he accelerated and once again swerved in front of the officer's vehicle. They continued in this manner, each weaving back and forth across both lanes of traffic; each trying to gain advantage over the other. Every near encounter produced a litany of curses and threats. Both had seemingly forgotten their larger purpose on the road at this hour.

Finally, both stopped at a light. Neither could contain the animosity any longer, and they bailed from their vehicles to crash together in a snarling confrontation. One of the two flung a fist, and soon thereafter the men were grappling and then rolling back and forth on Erdman Avenue, with traffic stopped around them. The off-duty officer was armed, and at some point the weapon tumbled from his holster and lay on the street, where his assailant picked it up. They struggled for possession of the weapon. Witnesses heard a single shot, and the civilian clutched his middle and sank to the asphalt. Medics pronounced him dead at the scene.

Tabeling examined the scene and spoke to witnesses, some of whom swore the officer had shot the man as he lay prostrate on the ground. As he studied the scene meticulously, he determined the angle of the projectile and of the entry wound. It was obvious the victim had been lunging at the prostrate officer—from above. That made it self-defense. Facts beat street emotions.

Crime scenes and what they evidenced had immersed Tabeling from his first one. Each scene was unique; each demanded meticulous scrutiny. Clues did not announce their significance or even their existence. Examining a scene took knowledge and procedure; legal strictures had to be adhered to. It took patience and persistence and, perhaps most of all, intuition, a feel for things—what fit in each scene and what did not; how certain parts of an investigation fit together. And then there was the total absorption of the facts and impressions that merged into an image far more complex than a jigsaw—like a three-dimensional game board constantly rotating on an axis and bathing in a varying intensity of light. Impressions then marinated within the brain, which might or might not produce a clear vision of the truth.

Steve was catching on to the creativity the job entailed. The clarity of thought. The incredible drive it demanded of all of them. And each case brought new challenges and new insights. Homicide was a learning laboratory made possible by legions of misfortunates who crossed at the wrong light, or pissed off the wrong guy, or looked at the wrong woman and who thereby became deceased. And the bloodshed never ceased. There also were other serious crimes: legions of rapes and robberies. For a student of violent crime, Baltimore was a graduate college of carnage.

No week went by without a unique challenge. A jewelry store holdup in well-heeled Howard County unleashed a torrent of mishaps as the fleeing robbers, with hostages in tow, jumped into a police car left at the intersection by responding officers—obligingly with keys in its ignition. Squealing tires broadcast their impending escape, but officers shot the rubber off their tires and forced the thieves to abandon that vehicle and commandeer another. A chase ensued at breakneck velocities, north on the interstate. The robbers, with their hostages, traded shots with a bevy of county officers. All vehicles headed toward Baltimore. The suspect vehicle was pulled over inside the beltway at Security Boulevard, where more shots were exchanged after a county officer mounted the suspect vehicle's trunk lid and fired into the passenger compartment. The driver, wounded in the buttock, attempted to exit the vehicle but was blocked by a county officer wielding a shotgun. The officer jammed the muzzle of the weapon into the vehicle, where the remaining thug clutched it and pulled on it, causing it to discharge, killing a hostage. Later, county police officers claimed the errant shot had been fired from a city police officer's weapon. Steve Tabeling's minute examination of the blast and its effects disproved the possibility of such a scenario. The state's attorney concurred.

In another bizarre case, one night a police officer's attention was riveted by the sight of a nude woman as she sprinted down her steps and across the street in front of his patrol vehicle, screaming, "Help! He raped me!" The officer caught up to the distraught woman, shepherded her to his vehicle, and instructed her to stay there. She pointed out the suspect, and the officer was radioing in the incident when he was confronted by the man. When the officer ordered the man to submit, the man assaulted the officer, and the two fell to the sidewalk, struggling. The man's size and strength forced the officer to shoot him. The alleged assailant was dead at the scene. As backup units arrived, the officer directed that the crime scene be secured. Then he returned to his vehicle and to the victim—but she had fled and was nowhere to be seen.

Tabeling's investigation disclosed that the deceased man had been the boyfriend of the woman. The two had engaged in sex, and as he had dressed to leave, she sprang from the house without warning, ran into the street, and shrieked to a passing police car that she had been assaulted. The state's attorney agreed no further prosecution would be constructive.

In another case, a number of women awaiting a bus after leaving work were accosted, dragged into nearby buildings, forced to disrobe, and sexually assaulted. Tabeling was asked to assist officers in apprehending the rapist. Beginning with examination of the area, he directed his detectives to interview workers, residents, bus drivers, and riders. Descriptions were given and compared. Without a staff artist to create a suspect likeness, Tabeling asked an acquaintance, an artist, if he might help. For twenty-five dollars, he created an image of the likely attacker. Dozens of the pictures were reproduced and displayed throughout the area. At headquarters, with the help of a makeup artists, detectives were selected to outfit themselves like potential victims to work as decoys, attempting to lure the attacker into striking. Shortly thereafter, the attacks ceased, and the rapist was apprehended, tried, and convicted. When the local paper reproduced the rapist's photo next to the artist's image, they were virtually identical. Teamwork, creativity, attention to detail, and leadership could overcome seemingly insurmountable problems. And some of the made-up male detectives in drag might just have fooled the rapist. They certainly elicited their share of wolf whistles and catcalls from their colleagues in the squad room.

A particularly gruesome double murder occurred when a drug-crazed addict forced himself into the office of a neighborhood dentist and demanded narcotics. When he was refused, the man bludgeoned the dentist with a metal bar. While searching the office for drugs, he discovered the terrified dental assistant, who had hidden herself inside a cabinet. Now thoroughly enraged, the intruder beat her to death as well. At that point, the woman's husband entered the office, curious why his wife had not met him in front of the building. He too was savagely beaten, though he survived. Frenzy sated, the killer left the building in the bloody shambles his rage had unleashed.

Methodical examination of the crime scene by homicide detective John Hess uncovered evidence—a broken piece of metal used in the attack. Marks on the metal indicated a drill bit might have been used on it, and the marks appeared to Hess to bear a distinctive pattern. After speaking to one of his informants about the case, Hess was put on to a particularly bad-tempered addict with whom the informant was acquainted, someone who might well be capable of committing such a brutal crime. When the detective mentioned the distinctive marking, the man told Hess that the suspect owned a shotgun with a broken stock that had been drilled and repaired, and he thought the work bore a similar characteristic mark.

With a suspect named, Tabeling assisted Hess in writing the search-and-seizure affidavit. Inside the addict's apartment, the two located the repaired shotgun and seized it. Tabeling then brought the item to crime lab technician Joe Reitz, a veteran firearms examiner and accomplished investigator in his own right, asked if the distinctive marking might be unique to that drill bit and traceable to the manufacturer, Reitz, aware that the FBI lab had responded to the same request with a polite refusal as not feasible, took the piece and conducted numerous tests and comparisons. He soon discovered that tool and die manufacturers transferred markings in the manufacturing process that were as distinct to each piece as the grooves inscribed inside the barrels of firearms. The lab results indicated a match, and that match placed their suspect at the murder scene on the day of occurrence. Imagination, good observation, cooperation, and logical thinking took a very dangerous man off the streets.

Another killer left behind a Pall Mall cigarette, broken in half, next to his victim. A tip led detectives to a suspect, where a search warrant discovered, among other incriminating evidence, broken cigarettes of the same brand and a newly opened pack on the suspect. When asked, he explained that he was trying to quit, and breaking each fresh one in half and tossing it was his special aid to get him to cessation. It got him to prison instead.

Most years there was nearly a murder a day. Unfortunates were found in every pathetic position, in every neighborhood of the city. They were found swollen and disfigured after a week in the harbor, bloated in abandoned houses, in shallow graves or burned-out car wrecks, in towed vehicles, in culverts or sewers, in torched buildings, and in collapsed structures. They were shot, stabbed, bludgeoned, strangled, drowned, or run over. It was, by any measure, a depressing litany of pain and suffering, and the detectives, all the cops and medics, and the crime scene techs had to steel themselves to it, no matter how gross or how ripe or how pitiful. It was their job. It was the work they were put on the earth to do, like it or not. And the piteous procession proceeded.

Sgt. Frank Grunder was enjoying a rare day off with his family. The commander of the Escape and Apprehension Squad, one of the hand-picked detectives selected to do the dangerous and dirty work of getting dangerous criminals off the city's streets, was with his wife and three children. They were driving south on Harford Road, nearing Saint Dominic's Catholic Elementary School, where Grunder had attended. Stopping at the red light at Echodale, Grunder was riveted by the sight of a wanted felon standing in the bus stop—a man sought in a citywide alert as an extremely dangerous criminal from the West Coast.

Sergeant Grunder took off on the green light and drove his family several blocks south to safety. He told his wife, Beverly, he would be a few minutes, and then he sprinted across the street to a pay phone to summon assistance. On the way, he was able to flag down a Northeastern District radio car, and he jumped in, explaining the situation to the officer as they sped north. Reaching the man's location, both officers jumped from the vehicle. Grunder, in civilian clothes, displayed his badge and ID and pointed his pistol at the man, ordering him to stand still. Ignoring the officer's command, the man turned and started to walk briskly away from the officers. The movement gave the man enough time to retrieve a handgun from his waist. He turned abruptly and fired one shot as Grunder neared him, hitting the sergeant in the chest. He was subdued by the uniformed officer.

Sergeant Grunder died on the school grounds where he had played as a child. He was laid out at the funeral home directly across the street.

The police commissioner directed Lt. Steve Tabeling to stand in attendance at the viewing of Sergeant Grunder for each of the days to show the department's deep sorrow and respect for his passing. On one of the evening viewings, Tabeling watched sadly as Sergeant Grunder's beautiful blonde daughter climbed up on the kneeler and stretched her child's form, reaching up to touch his badge and stroke his face. Tabeling had to leave the viewing room at that moment.

No day was an easy day for the detectives. Each brought new victims, new scenes, and new visits to the medical examiner and hospital ERs. Facts from yesterday's case percolated and awaited resolution. Tabeling made it his business not to micromanage, but at the same time, he would be there to assist if the workload threatened to overwhelm his detectives.

As a manager must, Tabeling came to perceive the large picture and understand that the mosaic of unfortunate victims represented not just a moment's violence and savagery but the culmination of a frothing river of emotions, disappointments, losses, and frustrations overflowing the banks and occasionally drowning innocents. He saw that every crime scene was a look into the mind and soul of the killer and that it begged the question: What kind of person could do such a thing? This, in turn, led him to formulate a hypothesis of the murdered and the murderer, a philosophy to explain and ultimately solve the crime. He thought thus to laser focus his skills as he continued in the important work of tracking killers.

In 1973, he received his Bachelor of Science degree from Loyola, one of the first in his family ever to graduate college. Without pausing for rest or refit, the seventh-grade dropout decided to enter the master's program there to study psychology. Exactly two years later, he was awarded an MS degree in psychology, a singular achievement. That accomplishment only whetted his appetite for more. Without hesitation, he immediately enrolled in a thirty-credit advanced graduate program in psychology. Steve Tabeling found himself smitten with higher education.

CHAPTER

12

T here was an anticipatory buzz among the normally placid elderly residents as the seventeen-piece dance band assembled its bandstand, sheet music stands, and seating in preparation for their concert. It was very seldom when anyone came to their nursing home to entertain them, and any attention was a special treat. As the musicians brought their instruments up to play, a hush fell over the residents. Then, suddenly, the brass and reeds erupted into "In the Mood," a 1940s Jimmy Dorsey smash, and the residents were instantly transformed back into toe-tapping, animated youths once again, some rising to embrace and waltz onto the dance floor. The second number was Glenn Miller's "Moonlight Serenade," which produced tears of recognition and joyful memories.

The band comprised trombones and clarinets, saxophones, drums, a bass fiddle, and of course trumpets, one of which was expertly played by Steve Tabeling. Glancing over the top of his sheet music, he glimpsed the residents dancing in place or with a partner to the intoxicatingly nostalgic rhythms as they engulfed them in waves of melodic and syncopated sound. For the elderly men and women, the years eroded and sweet memories and emotions flooded back.

Tabeling had never abandoned his music. Even as a police officer, he had volunteered his expertise to Saint Dominic's Drum Corps and was avidly accepted. He taught the youths how to produce sweet sounds from their instruments—how to hold them, care for them, and—the crowning achievement—how to decode the mysterious language known as sheet music. It was a transformative experience for all of them. They progressed then from rote memorizers of sounds to artists and musicians capable of a nuanced and bravura performance.

As the decade approached its halfway mark, Tabeling extended himself to achieve in the workplace, ensuring the maximum clearance rates and arresting the vicious killers that haunted his city and terrified neighborhoods. It was a sacred trust with his family, not only to provide them a good life but to make sure they each got a good education, attended mass each Sunday, and got enough exercise and good food. Honey was the architect of their home life, ever safeguarding them to ensure they had enough of everything, especially love and reassurance.

Steve attended regular night classes on the Loyola campus, and no night's instruction was an easy road, especially after a draining and demanding day responding to one crisis after another and juggling human resources to meet emerging crises. Tired he might be, but he was determined to see the thing through. It was his hallmark to never surrender his goals; to persevere with his course load, regardless of fatigue or discouragement. Attending night school while working a demanding job as manager of highly talented detectives, themselves often exhausted, and compelled to perform was not an occupation for the faint of heart.

And perform he did, supervising crime scene searches to comply with legalities necessary for convictions. He also directed crime lab technicians to properly photograph the scene. Throughout these processes, he always kept in mind the proper chain of custody on all evidence. Under Steve's supervision, detectives developed and interviewed witnesses. Detectives were also supervised when making sense of all evidence collected for presentation in a court of law.

He emphasized the need for a marriage between the Medical Examiner and State's Attorney for convictions. The detectives were directed to share all aspects of the investigation with the State's Attorney and Medical Examiner during the investigation. Attending autopsies was a must for first hand knowledge of cause and manner of death. The investigators dealt with the aggrieved, mournful, and vengeful families. They prepared for and appeared in court, sometimes waiting eight hours or more to testify in a case twelve months old, only to hear it had been postponed yet again.

And then on to the next one, subdued and sleep-deprived though they might be. They worked in a hushed avalanche of silent thought, logic, and deduction, plowing occasionally amid the boisterous and practical-joking crew that staffed Tabeling's shift, each a thoroughly unique individual and each as irreplaceable as a starting NFL quarterback.

There was tall, serious Steve Danko, ever dependable; Howard Corbin, a success story from west Baltimore, always willing to learn; Joe Thomas, a go-getter, the very kind of performer every shift needed; Augie Buchheit, a solid investigator; Ron La Martina, unflappable, warm, and perpetually smiling; and Ron Kincaid, sandy-haired, affable, a good communicator, and mentor to some of the other detectives. Together, they were more than the sum of their parts. They united whenever necessary to problem solve on a group level and then broke into pairs to canvas neighborhoods or shooting scenes and to locate witnesses, family members, and suspects. They, with the other members, worked murders like the proficient experts they were, but they worked kidnappings as well and sex crimes, extortions, and police-involved shootings. Each man possessed the uncanny ability to sift the evidence and separate fact from fiction, producing evidence and corroborating evidence in the process statements.

In a grim business, they were a joy to work alongside, and Tabeling frequently found himself jumping in to help out, much to his captain's chagrin. The workload did not permit any prima donnas. And the output—their month-to-month efficiency and production—was reported in writing all the way to the police commissioner, figures he scrutinized and could cite. It was an extraordinary month when their combined clearances dipped below 90 percent; with a conviction rater even higher.

They were an eclectic group, and each had made his way to Homicide by some convoluted path of achievement, recognition, or self-sacrifice. They were as irreverent as schoolboys and as dedicated as monks. And Tabeling was their acknowledged leader, not because of the certificate on his wall that said so but because of his knowledge of the job, of their working conditions, and of them. He was, after all, a street cop. It also was because of his level-headedness. He was never one to jump to conclusions or jump the gun. He was an assertive, confident leader who always seemed to have the answer or know where to get it. He was a confidant of state's attorneys, big bosses, and even judges and seemingly was esteemed by all. He was a gentlemen who knew the law, policy, procedure, and his personnel. Quiet yet not shy, he always was able and willing to rein in even the most bull-headed of them but in a way that was not in the least demeaning. It was more paternal reassurance that his proposed way would bring productive results.

And the detectives were as vital to the life of the city of Baltimore as fire fighters, public works employees, doctors and nurses, and transit workers. In fact, they were the most vital players, for without them the murderers that stalked the streets—predators, the kind that caused life on earth to devolve to a dark age—would go undetected and unpunished and remain free to kill others. So they worked to exhaustion for the good of everyone.

By 1974, disgusted police employees, increasingly frustrated by the city's parsimonious or nonexistent annual raises, got permission to affiliate themselves with a national labor union. Union leadership tried several ploys to garner guaranteed pay raises, but faced with a city government chronically cash-deprived, none of their efforts bore fruit. Perhaps to placate their workers' frustrations, the employee organization leadership tried a more draconian strategy. Planned with D-Day secrecy and exquisite timetables and absent tangible results on the negotiation front, the plan was scheduled to unfold in the mid-evening shift on the seventh day of July—the peak of the violent street crime "season."

As the initial start of their strike, they selected a police district known as problematic even during quiet times. The Southwestern District was home to about 11 percent of the city's population. It abutted the high-crime Western District, with much attendant violent crime spill-over and a crazy-quilt street network best described as chaotic, the consequence of its creation as a series of adjacent small towns, industrial areas, and aging houses built at crazy angles without regard to twentieth-century highways. Thus, only indigenously assigned patrol officers truly understood how to get from point A to B because usually no straight line between them existed. The district was peopled by multiple ethnicities, many of whom regarded police as a distasteful presence in their communities. The people were as likely to greet a responding officer with a right cross as an extended hand. In some respects, it was a region of the city that had failed to keep pace with progress. It kept its own seasons, logic, and practices, many of which dated to pre-Civil War days. And on summer evenings, it was a very busy place to be a cop.

On that evening, calls for service were running normal for a summer three-to-eleven shift, which normally comprise about 43 percent of a district's total dispatched workload. There were, as always, a certain percentage of junk calls—man seeking assistance, disorderly juveniles, flooded basement, and such—but the southwest side of the city produced its share of serious crimes: assault in progress, breaking and entering, stolen autos. What imparted a sense of security to the residents was the assurance that a police officer was one 911 call away. Indeed, most district patrol shift officers prided themselves on a prompt response to any call for help; usually, an officer showed up within minutes. It was the kind of unspoken accord between citizens and the police; a "we'll be there for you" bond.

On the chosen night, the shift officers reported; stood roll call; got their radios, batteries, car keys, and assignments; and left to drive to their respective posts. As the tide of 911 calls came in and began to swell, the calls were handled as expeditiously as always. Absolutely no reason for alarm was apparent.

Then, according to a prearranged plan, at 2000 hours, all the patrol cars pulled into predesignated and strategically located parking lots, parked the vehicles in neat rows, turned their radios off, and tossed them and the car keys into each vehicle's trunk and slammed it shut. The officers then boarded a bus, which drove them to a meeting destination, as planned. Southwestern District, all twelve square miles of it, was completely without police protection. For the first time in its history, Baltimore police officers had abandoned their posts and turned their backs on their sacred sworn duty.

The district communications dispatcher at headquarters, privy to none of this, continued to receive and dispatch the flood of calls that were normal for that time of the evening, calls that grew in volume and urgency.

"831, 831. I have a cutting in progress at Edmondson and Branch. 831, can you respond? 831 is 10-5—not responding. 835? 835, can you respond to a cutting in progress at that 10-20? 835? 835 is also 10-5."

The dispatcher then attempted to call the squad supervisor, but the sergeant had departed with his officers. The entire shift was no longer there.

As the severity of the crisis seeped into the consciousness of the command ranks, first at the communications division, appropriate notifications were made: on-call duty officer, chief of the patrol division, subordinate commanders, and, of course, with trepidation, the police commissioner.

"Sir, sorry to bother you, but there seems to be a problem in one of the districts. They are not responding to calls for service. Yes, the equipment is fine—we checked. Yes, sir, we're notifying the tactical commander to shift his officers to the affected area at least until we can find out what the problem is."

The Tactical Section worked all high-crime areas in supplement to district patrol units in an ongoing effort to suppress street crimes. They were handpicked for the assignment and were considered to be the very best motivated of the patrol division. They were a supplement and, in this case, a reserve force to backfill southwestern posts and handle the rising backlog of calls, at least until the situation could be straightened out.

When called, however, they failed to answer their radios. In fact, they no longer could answer them since they were locked in the trunks of their vehicles, and the tactical squads were on their way to a meeting location to wait out the anticipated storm. Later, officers from both commands would don cardboard signs proclaiming the unfairness of the city of Baltimore and the Baltimore Police Department to their employees.

To his everlasting credit, Pomerleau was quick to read the signs, evaluate the situation and, most of all, to react decisively. Lieutenants and higher from the entire 3,200-member department were called, most of them at home, and instructed to contact all their personnel, have them don full uniforms, including riot gear, and get to the HQ auditorium for 2100 hours roll call. It was unprecedented, and it did two things; it put everybody on notice that (1) the former marine colonel was not going to take this lightly, and (2) those who failed to respond to this call in the department's time of pressing need would declare their disloyalty for all to see, a fact that would be duly noted once the present situation was rectified.

Meanwhile, intelligence units were culling information from every assignment in the city: who was in and how many were out? By the time of the roll call, the department had counted over one thousand strikers. It was a breathtaking betrayal of the oath of office and the citizens of Baltimore. But it was a figure that could be managed. That many out meant that nearly twice that many were ready to go. As the minutes ticked by, word on the streets of Baltimore was that there were no cops on the streets. Anything went—and it shortly did, as thousands of celebrants, arsonists, thieves, and thugs swarmed the nearest commercial areas in an orgy of smash, grab, burn, and go. As the first respondents to the commissioner's call stood awaiting roll call start, on the fifth floor mezzanine outside of the auditorium, orange flames illuminated the eastern sky, lit by blazing stores on east Baltimore Street. A similar scene greeted westward-facing spectators looking down west Baltimore Street. To the northwest, Oldtowne Mall, lovingly restored to its former nineteenth-century elegance after its rough treatment during the 1968 riots, once again blossomed brightly in lurid yellow and orange blazes. By morning, it would be finished for good.

As the hour neared for the gathering of the loyal officers, the huge auditorium filled with blue uniforms. It sat 494 persons, but when Tabeling arrived with his men, he estimated that there were easily more than six hundred already inside, with more coming. Some earliest responders to the call had already been briefed and dispatched to areas of the city deemed most needed.

And tempers were already smoldering among the officers, most of whom had already worked a full shift—if not more—and were contemplating bed when roused. At this stage there was absolutely no necessity for commanders to whip up animosity for the strikers; it grew spontaneously among the officers. Detectives, especially those assigned to murders, were particularly livid. They already were burdened with impossible workloads and recognized they would slide further behind any possibility of garnering clearances or making arrests while this abortion of a strike continued. The murmuring from hundreds of angry men and women was growing in intensity, like summer winds before a storm. Then, in an instant, perfect silence was restored.

"Detail!" barked the voice. *"Atten-shun!"*

As one being, over six hundred police officers rose to their feet and stood at rigid attention.

Pomerleau entered from the right and strode to the center of the enormous stage. He was one immensely powerful man who felt every eye upon him. "As you were," he growled, and all who had seats took them.

He gazed at the impressive audience of dark blue before him. Though it was not possible to suppose his thoughts, the spectacle of his department—his loyal members—rallied around during this severe crisis must have given him some sliver of satisfaction. The conflict had scarcely begun, but he could see before him the means by which the opposition—and he thought of the strikers as dishonorable, traitorous adversaries—would be utterly crushed.

He went on to brief them on the situation; it was an economical update that spelled out the situation as it was understood at that hour, as well as what he planned to do about it. As it turned out, plans for deployment were even then being finalized. Only half of the available loyal officers had been told to respond that evening. The officers present would be deployed as vehicles were made available—three, sometimes four to a police car. Normally the on-street evening shift of the city would comprise about 220 officers, plus supervisors and tactical units—three hundred all told. Now Pomerleau planned— by use of twelve-hour shifts, canceled days off and annual leave, and other economies—to field about a thousand on each of two shifts, more than tripling the normal complements. He instructed the loyal members not to take any abuse from the strikers—or from anyone. They were to respond safely, aggressively where necessary, and to "do what's necessary to fulfill your responsibilities." The implications were clear, and many nodded in silent assent. From those first moments, it was obvious to all that they were going to triumph over the strikers. *Those poor bastards*, many thought.

The officers were assigned to one of the eight striking districts, and their commanders and sergeants set about organizing transport. The remaining district, Eastern, a tight-knit group known for their district solidarity, had taken a vote. "We all go out," said the spokesman to the assembled cops, "or we all stay and work!" The vote was unanimous, save one officer who opted to strike, and the officers of the indomitable Eastern District would neither ask for nor accept any outside help for the duration of the strike, epitomizing *espirit*.

Tabeling was assigned his own detectives and those of another lieutenant. They were thirty-eight in number, and they were ordered to take care of business in the Western District, one of the epicenters of embryonic street insurrection, in addition to its labor issues. As a former transit operator, Steve took the wheel of the department bus, a decrepit conveyance normally parked in the corner shadows of the underground motor pool garage. It started with some effort, coughed out its most recent fumes, and, balking like a grouchy animal, crept up the exit ramp and onto the street, where it was boarded by the detectives, some of whom were responding to the crisis like kids on a field trip. When everyone, along with their riot helmets, batons, and shields, was loaded, their driver lieutenant muscled the clutch to the floor, pulled the antiquated shifter into first, and turned west onto Fayette Street.

The bus crept along at ten miles an hour, obviously its maximum velocity, and Tabeling grew concerned as they approached Gay Street, which led to the up ramp that led across the Orleans Street viaduct, a magnificent elevated roadway that arched over part of the downtown area. As he feared, the old transport sputtered, shuddered violently, and coughed but kept up its pace until they reached the red light at the eastern end, prior to turning west onto Franklin Street. When the light flashed green, Tabeling eased the clutch out and slid the stick into first gear, only to have the rickety engine sputter and die.

Had the situation not been so critical, it would have been humorous. No amount of key turning, accelerator pumping, or choke pulling could coax the engine back to life. Humiliatingly, thirty-eight of Baltimore's best cops were stranded at the end of the Orleans Street viaduct, stared at by drivers and pedestrians, who, in turn, the stranded angry cops glared at.

Tabeling was accustomed to conveyances powered by electricity and riding rails, and he could think only of lightening the load. He suggested they all get out and push the stalled vehicle. With remarkable good grace, they did so, probably realizing that it was better to do something rather than blocking a lane of traffic. Thirty-eight uniformed police officers, some of the city's finest investigators among them, put their backs and shoulders and rusty muscles to the task. Tabeling remained in the driver's seat, shifter firmly in hand and in neutral, clutch held to the floor, and on his signal, all heaved. They let out a collective groan, but the ancient bus began to roll forward up the slight incline. As they reached what Tabeling considered to be maximum speed, he popped the clutch, and the ancient engine sputtered to life. The men let out a ragged hurrah and jogged to catch and board. In a minute or two, they were again on their way to confront the challenges ahead at embattled Western.

The Western District station house sat on Riggs and Mount Streets, surrounded by a neighborhood usually described as "disadvantaged." One of the few district houses adjacent to residences, it had the advantage of being accessible to the neighbors, many of whom did not drive. On the first night of the strike, many of them availed themselves of this convenience and congregated in a noisy, milling crowd outside of the district. Across the street from them and opposite the station, Western District officers participating in the strike congregated as well. There was a mutual antipathy between the two groups, fueled, no doubt, by previous run-ins and exacerbated by the late hour and the fact that many of the officers, wearing whole or partial versions of their uniforms, weapons included, had been drinking for some time. A few beer cans whacked against the side of the bus as Tabeling turned the vehicle off Riggs to pull onto the lot. The strikers erupted in abuse.

"Scab fucks!" one yelled. "Good luck finding car keys!" shrieked another as he tossed a handful of departmental key rings onto neighboring roofs. Similar epithets emanated from the others, along with more tossed empties. Steve calmly pulled the vehicle onto the lot, closest to the building, and instructed his officers to exit the bus and enter to avoid any confrontations. They weren't quick enough, as one of the detectives was struck in the face and turned to confront the offender. Tabeling turned him around and gently propelled him to the station door. Across the street, emboldened by the actions of the strikers, some residents began tossing items as well, most of which fluttered harmlessly to the asphalt.

After being briefed by the district commander, Tabeling talked to his officers, reminding them of the importance of staying calm and avoiding any incidents with the Western men. "Of course defend yourself, if you need to," he told them, "but let's focus on what we are here to do, what these people have refused to do: their jobs."

With that, he bade them stand by and then walked onto the parking lot and straight toward the strikers, many wearing their cardboard placards. Hostility radiated from a dozen of them. But there were other men there who Tabeling had worked beside. As he neared them, ten or more stepped toward him expectantly. Rather than engage, they listened.

"Look," he began, "I know you've got grievances. We all know that. But"—he raised his hand palm upward—"this is not the way to be heard; believe me. I just left the police commissioner. If you know anything about the man, you've got to know this: He is not the kind of man who is going to take this lying down."

Several of the striking officers looked at the ground as they heard Steve's words. One nodded slowly.

"Put yourselves in his shoes. He can't let you win. Not this way." Steve frowned and shook his head. "All of you need to stop this now, get your gear, and come back to work."

They hesitated, and several exchanged concerned glances.

"I'm telling you for your own good." Tabeling buttressed his persuasive logic. "This man will fire you! Do not doubt that!" He turned and reentered the district. His men prepared to get on to their posts.

It was the beginning of five contentious twelve-hour days. At the end of each, the exhausted detectives returned to the Western station, relieved by another twelve-hour contingent. Often too exhausted even to eat, they made their way to the rec room to drop onto a creaky army cot, one of dozens that had been assembled and set out for the use of the troops. Most were asleep before their eyes closed.

At headquarters by the second day, Pomerleau, reacting as the savvy field commander he was, determined to institute two initiatives that were aimed at destroying the union's capabilities and cohesion. He inquired of his fiscal director as to the mechanics involved in disrupting the labor organization's dues check-off capabilities—the faucet that poured funds into its coffers around the clock. The commissioner directed that the privilege be revoked, and it immediately was. The union would be forced to prosecute its illegal strike without the benefit of any local dollars.

Then, turning his attention to the demographic characteristics of the thousand-plus men and women on the picket lines, he focused principally on one age group. "Tell me," he said, "how many of them are on probation?"

Getting that information took a bit of doing, but the number was in excess of 130 thirty who had not yet attained seniority and protection from summary disciplinary action under Maryland law.

"Fire them," he said.

The officers seated before him let out an audible gasp. *Never* had a police commissioner done a wholesale firing. When word got out of the unprecedented number of terminations—as it was enthusiastically intended to—with zero threats, no warning, no by your leave or kiss my ass, waves of disbelief, revulsion, and, most desired of all by commanders, *fear* swept through the department and swamped the ranks of those on strike. They were reminded that their actions were illegal and that they had breached their sworn duty to preserve, protect, and defend. It was a sacred oath sworn before God. Pomerleau's decisive—some might say brutally effective—actions did much to deflate any confidence the strikers might have felt. After all, they had trusted the union leadership. Those guys were players on a national level; they were winners, weren't they? Maybe. But they had never encountered a man like Donald Pomerleau.

From the time of his decision, working police officers began to receive calls via communications, such as, "Any unit in the vicinity of Westside Shopping Center. Meet a man requesting information." Responding units would be met by two or more former strikers turned out in clean, pressed uniforms and eager to return to duty. In deference to their reticence at being spotted and targeted by officers still on the picket line, the cruising patrol was requested. Enclosed, they rode in anonymity into the station lot to pick up their assignment, car keys, radio, and fresh batteries and then went out through the picket line, taking their chances like everybody else, and out onto their post assignment.

Thus, each night the on-street strength of the police department grew, until some of the highest-crime and workload districts were bulging with three-officer cars, and requests for police assistance might fetch a dozen or more officers, now fast growing restive with not enough work. They were augmented by dozens of Maryland State Police who entered the city and responded to in-progress calls in convoys. The Baltimore Police Motorcycle Unit, sixty or so burly leather-jacketed and helmeted officers, likewise kept the capability to converge at a hot call in a thunderous, roaring symphony, reminiscent of a motorcycle gang movie. As spectacle, it was most impressive.

There was one other issue. On the second day, the Baltimore City Jail Corrections Officers Association opted to stage its own wildcat strike, and every jail guard trooped out of the institution, leaving more than two thousand inmates, many of them violent felons, completely to their own devices. Most were not sealed in cells but allowed the virtual freedom of the institution. Pomerleau responded to that crisis as well, peeling off several hundred of his officers under a particularly confrontational colonel, with directions to restore order forthwith. In company with several dozen K-9 teams, German shepherds predominating, order was restored.

The strike waned after five days, and then collapsed. Strong leadership, sternly administered, had won out. The inner-city neighborhoods smoldered longer, long after the fires had been extinguished. It was as if there had been a fundamental breach of trust between the city government, their employees, the employee organizations, and some of the residents. It was as if those essential strands of society had been unraveled, and that the important element—trust—the very weave of social fabric, had been dissolved. The question was how to ever get it back.

CHAPTER

13

By the end of five days, it was almost a pleasure for Lieutenant Tabeling and his exhausted detectives to return to their desks and begin handling normal workload once more. Perhaps it was a sad commentary of life in Baltimore, but at least a man knew what to expect from a violent felon. The business of these detectives was investigating murders, and, sadly, business was good.

Not all of the killings were confined to back alleys, parking garages, and bars. One day in early April, Charles Hopkins, an infuriated business owner, stomped into the temporary City Hall, demanding to see Mayor William Donald Schaefer. His business had been shuttered by an inability to obtain necessary city permits, and he was determined to wrest satisfaction from the politician he viewed as responsible. His previous attempts by mail and telephone had garnered him no satisfaction. So today he meant to air his grievances in person on the mayor.

Somewhat out of the ordinary was the fact that he carried a .38 caliber revolver, concealed in his clothing, and managed to gain entry without the weapon being discovered.

The mayor's offices temporarily resided on the seventh floor of the prosaic poured-concrete building. As he progressed from entry upward, the man's behavior deteriorated, and he grew more agitated. The first elected government official he encountered was Councilman Dominic Leone, a gregarious man who approached him to direct and assist him. Hopkins, growing increasingly restive and perhaps perceiving that this man was part of the machinations that had blocked him in the past, fired two shots that struck Leone in the midsection, wounds that would prove to be fatal. He then shot Councilman Carroll J. Fitzgerald in the chest. A third councilman, confronted by the gunmen, experienced a sharp sensation of chest pain, presaging a heart attack, and crumpled to the marble floor.

Soon after, Hopkins was met by the receptionist, Kathleen Nolan, who, no doubt, had more than an inkling that huge trouble was coming her way, though she confronted it nonetheless. "Put that gun away," she ordered. When no response was forthcoming, she pressed on. "Who are you?" she asked. "What are you doing here?" Her courage and defiance confounded Hopkins, and he emitted a stream of profanity, garnishing it with still another shot that struck Ms. Nolan in the chest.

Unsuccessful at gaining entrance, he turned to leave and, with another blast of profanity, warned the injured woman, "I'm coming back."

The gunshots set off alarms, and police officers assigned to the City Hall came dashing. Workers for the city government scurried to find safety, and calls were hurriedly placed to police headquarters requesting immediate assistance. Still in the process of forming a SWAT organization, Baltimore Police Tactical officers responded under their commanding officer and, with ad hoc teams quickly organized on the fly, rushed the intervening three blocks from headquarters to make entry. Once inside the huge structure, the officers could clearly hear gunshots. They quickly established a plan and began the perilous process of searching each floor and evacuating the casualties as each was encountered.

Tabeling was notified and responded as well, briefed as he arrived by the Tactical commander. As soon as practical, the police teams cleared each floor, encountering the seriously wounded Councilman

Leone and the severely stricken Councilman Curran. Ambulances were summoned, and the search teams continued. Hopkins was finally cornered in the office of the City Council president, where he resisted and was shot several times and captured. It was soon discovered that one of the security police officers, Thomas Gaither, had received a flesh wound—a ricochet some thought. He was treated at Mercy Hospital and released, as was the wounded receptionist and the surviving councilman, all of whom recovered. The gunman was admitted in critical condition.

That the incursion into City Hall sent shudders throughout city government was an understatement. Hopkins survived and was tried and convicted for the murder and the multiple shootings.

The City Hall skirmish was way out of the ordinary for any government entity, and the incident was impetus enough to cause security in public buildings to be seriously amped up in the coming years, a trend that seemed to anticipate future terrorist attacks.

For certain, the shooting mesmerized every strata of the police department as well, and no one had more pointed questions than Donald Pomerleau. Many of the questions would prove to be quite awkward for the security commander—beginning with, "How did a man with a gun waltz past the security checkpoint at the entrance?"—but were painfully fielded. The incident, tragic though it was, was also embarrassing. Baltimore couldn't keep gunmen off its streets, it seemed to say. *And now they can't keep them out of the seat of government!*

The buck stopped on Tabeling's desk, and he was left to assess, analyze, and report each minute of the gunman's actions, recording the complex sequence of his movements, crimes, and capture. That took many hours and many witness statements to sort out. The shooting happened on a Wednesday, and he had finally completed the gargantuan document by Friday morning and had returned home and climbed into bed for some much needed rest. Just as sleep overtook him, the phone rang.

It was Steve Danko, both apologetic and compelling. "I hate to bother you, Lieutenant," he began, "but we just got a call from a nut job in the southwest, we think. He says he's gonna start shooting up an intersection in west Baltimore about six. That's all he said."

Tabeling's brain transitioned from the meager level of shallow sleep he had just gotten to *all ahead full.* He stared at the nightstand for an instant, wondering what he could do about the situation from his bedroom, but like the professional he was, he replied sleepily that he would be in shortly, and they would see to it. He instructed Detective Danko to visit the Southern and Southwestern Districts to see if there was any report of an individual at serious odds with the police. He also told him to broadcast the information on the citywide channel.

That night the telephone caller made good on his word when he opened the second-floor front window of the three-story rowhouse on West Lombard Street and thrust his .30-30 rifle through the opening and aimed along its gleaming barrel to fire randomly at anyone he saw.

One of the first was a young police officer from the adjacent Western District, a marine combat veteran from Vietnam, who sped south on Carey Street as soon as communications dispatched the call, "Shots fired, Carey and Lombard! Shots fired!" As he passed the intersection, Officer Holcomb braked to a stop, exited, and took cover behind a car parked diagonally from the gunman's perch. As he raised his head above a parked vehicle roof to get a clear sight picture of the shooter, the eighteen-year-old, himself a National Guard-trained sniper and avid hunter, spotted him and fired one round, which pierced the roof of the car and buried itself in the throat of police officer Jimmy Holcomb, killing him instantly.

What ensued verged on pandemonium. Once the "Signal 13. Shots fired. Carey and Lombard. Officer down" transmission was broadcast and simulcast on the citywide channel, officers, regardless of their assignments, dropped what they were engaged in and floored accelerators, with lights and sirens activated, determined to get to the scene ASAP. Within twenty minutes, well over one hundred uniformed and plainclothes officers surrounded the sniper's perch. Four responding officers were also wounded and pinned down by the sniper after bravely attempting to reach Officer Holcomb. They persevered at the same location for two hours. During that time, over four hundred rounds were fired, most by the police. The suspect, John Earl Williams, surrendered about two hours after the first shot.

Tabeling's work was just beginning. For the next days, he worked around the clock, locating and interviewing witnesses. He collected more statements, studied the scene, examined evidence, and deducted motives and possibilities. That one officer had given his life was tragedy enough. That four more had nearly lost their lives was a potential epic disaster and had been narrowly averted by the quick thinking of the wounded officers themselves, who hunkered down, evading flying glass and the sonic cracks of bullets above their position.

When the documents were ready, Tabeling felt wrung out with exhaustion but knew he had thoroughly researched, investigated, and summarized the massive episode, one that would change the tactical approaches of the police department for generations to come. The City Hall shooting topped by the Lombard Street sniper had done much to anguish the city itself. The unprecedented violence of both events and their jarring juxtaposition staggered the city. Yet the department soldiered on, scarred by the incidents, to be sure, but as confident in themselves and their colleagues as ever—even more. They had survived the searing ordeals of illegal strikes, arsons and looting, attacks on the seat of government, and the deadly ambush of police officers rushing to the aid of others. Nothing had weakened them. The confrontations had made them stronger. They were Baltimore cops—none better.

14

A ny disruption of the normal ebb and flow of the pattern of the day could unsettle the rhythm of their work. After the tidal wave of the multiple police shootings, the job again returned to normal. Murders followed no pattern, but in Baltimore, bodies dropped with depressing regularity, leaving the eternally enervated detectives pacing themselves, pausing to collect their thoughts and finish their notes on the current investigation before plunging in on the new one. Each day, it seemed, more suspects were brought in. It was as though there was no limit on potential murderers in Baltimore.

It was not uncommon for a murder suspect to completely clam up when confronted by an investigator. Tabeling made himself available to his men for the most difficult suspects. He considered it a good sign to be asked and liked the challenge of a stonewaller, a clam. Such was the case of Tyrone Walters, a murder suspect brought in by uniformed officers and identified by a witness as the probable trigger-puller on a shooting death from last shift.

Tabeling observed the man as he sat stiffly in the straight-backed chair in the interview booth. It was not a comfortable chair—it required a rigid posture—but as a platform from which to observe a suspect, it served its purpose. The man looked straight ahead. His posture was stiff, and his face was drawn into a glaring mask of debased self-esteem. Like the portrait of a Bantu warrior chief, this one carried himself with flamboyant presence, even seated. This one would not be easy.

Tabeling was prepared for this. He observed the man and the exaggerated sense of his aggrieved dignity. He had sent two detectives to the man's haunts, where they spent hours of their valuable time rapping on doors, showing the suspect's image and asking who he was, who he associated with, how he lived, and more.

Steve's techniques had not been learned in textbooks. The psychology courses imparted many useful insights, but nothing taught better than the school of real life—observation, civility, and professional behavior. Control of the interview, the sequence of questions, their pace, and of the pressure applied—all of it was psychological. If he spoke, all the better. But if he clammed up, there were innumerable cues to invoke and observe. He looked very much in control.

Tabeling entered the small room, nodded to the man, and lay his notes on the table. They were written in looping, cursive letters, page after yellow legal page, line after line. It was bait to get the man to glimpse down, but he didn't bite. He stared straight ahead, as if he meant to laser a hole in the opposite wall.

"I'm Detective Lieutenant Steve Tabeling, and this is the Homicide Division. I guess you know what that means." It was another cast that hit only vapor. "I'd like you to tell me something about yourself. We know your name, of course, and that you live on East Thirty-First Street. That right?'

Nothing.

"I'd also like to hear if you have family. Is there anyone we can notify that you're going to be with us for a while?"

Again, nothing. Steve edged his chair over to the side a bit, so as to get into the man's direct vision. That way, it was harder for him to glare over Tabeling's shoulder. It worked. The man fixed his scowl just above the bridge of Tabeling's nose. There, the resentment smoldered like a glowing coal.

"I think you should know that I know quite a lot about you. Maybe a lot more than you think."

This connected but only for a fraction of a second. Then the glower returned.

"I know that last Wednesday night you were at the bar at Twenty-Sixth and Maryland. You go there a couple nights a week; that right? You sit with a man who used to work down the Point? Sam Freeman? You know him, right? He knows you. You drank with him until eleven or so and then went down the street to your woman's house. You like Wednesdays because her man has his little boy on those nights. Gives you some space. I understand that."

At this there was the slightest flicker of recognition and discomfort about the information this cop knew, but more about the intimacy of it. His eyes maintained their hard glare, but his torso rotated ever so briefly in the sturdy chair. It was a small, spontaneous movement of the body, possible involuntary, but it exhibited a trace of discomfort—an atom of *Oh, shit, what else do he know?'*

Steve plowed on. "That woman—she's Marilyn? She is quite a bit older than you, right? She been married—wait, this can't be right." Tabeling held the legal page higher above the table. "Says here *four* times? She's got children from three of these men? Mister, you are a *brave* soul! I have to ask you—does she badger you for child support? I mean, does she ever confuse you with one of the others?" Tabeling smiled good-naturedly as he said it. "Be perfectly natural, I guess."

For an instant, Walters lost his poise and began the perp's eye search for a soothing surface to stare at. His eyes circled in their orbits, hoping to focus on something calming for a break from this too-well-informed cop.

"Well," Tabeling continued, "does she know you got another woman down on North Avenue? In that second-floor apartment? And that she's expecting?"

Tabeling watched the man carefully—the bobbing apple in his throat, subtle yet there; the tightening forehead, like the taut skin on a snare drum. Still, his eyes were fixed, and he was giving nothing.

"Oh, by the way, if you feel the need to use the restroom or you want some water or something, happy to help." He smiled again pleasantly. "The men's room's right down the hall. 'Course, one of the detectives has to accompany you. You good?"

The man nodded imperceptibly, but it was a crack in the shell.

"Good," Steve said. "I need to talk to you about a murder that happened right around the corner from your girlfriend's house. That is, girlfriend number two. Happened about eleven last night. Man found with a gunshot wound. It turns out he used to drink with you and Sam at that bar? Robert Smith. Know him? 'Bout this tall; kind of stocky? Wore loud shirts? Do you know anybody who had anything against Mr. Smith? Seems to be a sad older man. Who would do a thing like that?" Nothing still, and yet there was a faint glimmer of … some emotion. Maybe he was not as iron-hard as his expression. Maybe he had some feelings for somebody else. Tabeling decided on another tack.

"You know we got a call from an older lady about an hour ago. Do you have an aunt who might be calling here? Elderly? She sounded upset. Asked about you by name. Mrs. Childs? Mrs. Ruth Childs?"

He saw at once he had struck a nerve. The man's face twitched once again. The glare melted into a cloud of confused, unfocused stares—first at his shoes, then the table leg, then his belt buckle. His forehead wrinkled. Then a major move—his body swiveled out of its discomforting rigidity into the merest sag. Not a word escaped, yet his language was a symphony nonetheless. "She's my granny," he said at last.

"And she raised you up, it says here. Took you in when your mother passed. Is that right?"

The man dropped his head onto his chest and nodded. "That's right, Officer. She raised me after my mama passed."

"Well, I thought you should know she sounded upset. You can call her later if you want. But first I'd like you to clarify some things for me. That be all right?"

And it was. And it confirmed several things Tabeling had learned and was learning about people: even hardened criminals have someone they want to please. Most of them don't want to hurt somebody who's been good to them. And the kicker was that deep down, everybody wants to tell their story. Everybody wants to get it off their chests to somebody. And Tabeling reasoned, *It might as well be me.*

Tyrone Walters told his story about how he and Mr. Smith got into a fight, fueled by beer and fanned by grievances, old and imagined. Bringing a gun to the bar was not a planned thing; he had wanted to sell it. None of it was planned, rather like Mr. Walters's entire life. And now Mr. Smith could rest in peace, grievances settled.

Knowledge. Observation. Leverage. All judiciously applied. Like working open a clam with persistence. Tirelessly.

Most people are good, Tabeling believed, but that small percentage will definitely go off the trail and kill for various reasons: greed, passion, drug-induced, or alcohol-fueled. It was what homicide cops existed for—to talk for the dead. To get justice for them. To deter future crimes. To balance the odds between good and evil. The handful of men Steve led were the thin line of heroes by anybody's standards. And they were very good at their chosen line of work.

The city never failed to produce criminal events that verged on the bizarre.

There was the case of the Coast Guardsman found severely beaten about the head. It might have been an unsolved case until an informant stepped up to enlighten the police about what actually happened. Seemed the deceased was out for a night when he was lured by a hotel bar doorman, who invited him to ride in his van, telling him they were going out to pick up some women. Once inside, the trap sprung, and the victim was brutally hammered on the head with a tire iron wielded by the now-aggressive doorman, who then pulled the unconscious man from the vehicle and onto the street, where he stomped him. Thanks to a prostitute nicknamed Horse-Face and the fact that the suspect was careless enough to order drinks later that night using a credit card with bloodstains on it, the detectives were able to pick up the six-foot Walter Fisher before the end of their shift.

Fisher claimed self-defense and said nothing more. Tabeling learned that a second person was in the van that night and that he had fled to Florida. Inquiries with the Florida State Police turned up his location: Clearwater. Together with Augie Buchheit, Steve flew there and took the man into custody for extradition. After a little coaxing, he admitted his role in the crime.

By the late '70s, Tabeling could feel a quiet pride in his career and his educational achievements but most of all in his family, his mainstay. After young Steve graduated from Calvert Hall, he entered Towson State, and in 1974, he began a sojourn into professional baseball. He attended the Baltimore Orioles and Pittsburgh Pirates training camps, but was not signed. After a few years trying baseball, Steve decided to join Johns Hopkins Hospital as an administrator, a career that would lead to his own business in the years to come.

Sondra, the oldest girl, was a married mother of two living in Pennsylvania.

Honey married a man who did very well in the construction industry and became a homemaker, raising three children.

Youngest Patty married a CPA, and they had four children together. Interested in all things of a medical nature, she received the required training and became a phlebotomist.

Steve's beloved wife, Honey, continued in her role as matriarch of the family and in her efforts to coach and pilot her husband over the shoals of grammar and sentence structure, even though he was, by then, a graduate student. "I liked you better when you were dumber," she told him.

When Steve's mother called to say that Steve's father was suffering from throat cancer—that he wouldn't eat and that she was going to have to put him in a nursing home—Honey quietly said, "He's not going in a nursing home." When she was informed that she didn't have the skills to care for a terminally ill man, she answered succinctly, "I can learn." And learn she did. Honey spent time at The Johns Hopkins Hospital learning how to insert, withdraw and clean a feeding tube, to suction his trach, partially disrobe and bathe him; keep him from getting bed sores by constant movement; and other crucial skills. Honey, ever the superb student, became a first-rate technician, and Steve's father, ever the contentious, scrappy one of the family, showed his appreciation for Honey's loving attention. He occasionally smiled at her, showing the peace that comes with receiving end-of-life care in the company of loved ones. Honey had done much the same for her husband's grandfather, years before, nursing him on his final journey.

The year 1977 was frenzied in the activities and in the issues thrown Steve's way. To his surprise, Pomerleau appointed him to attend the prestigious FBI National Academy in Quantico, Virginia. It was a demanding eleven-week course of study, offering a varied list of academic courses created for the criminal justice field, given under the auspices of the University of Virginia and dealing with multiple disciplines that were indispensable to modern law enforcement. Police leaders from across the United States and Western European departments attended. The attendees were handpicked—selection for attendance was a singular honor—and they represented the very best of their agencies.

Because Steve was already a graduate student, he was required to enroll in higher-level courses than the other students. But, as was his custom, he launched himself into the curriculum at full throttle and was soon immersed himself in topics dealing with forensics and, most especially prized, the law, and with it, case law. He immersed himself in the Carroll Doctrine, a Prohibition-era decision that allowed cops to stop and search cars with probable cause.

Listening to accomplished lecturers, Tabeling was able to grasp nuances of the law and the ways to comprehend, interpret, and apply it that he had never before appreciated. The law had been his first fascination with his profession and had played a major role in his ability to grasp complex concepts, interpret them, and put them into practical application on the street. He became adept at creating legal briefs, abbreviated versions of complicated cases that distilled the complexities of the case into relevant essences. It had proved to be a potent skill—the ability to apply logic to atrocious actions, wade through the horror, and unearth the material truth that would solve complex crimes and put the offender where he belonged.

Back in Baltimore, Steve was to learn that a scurrilous political attack had been launched against members of the department, motivated by that most insidious dark force: *ambition*. Two senior police officials vied and struggled to oust a respected member from his post as a high-ranking commander in the Criminal Investigation Division. Even more sinister, their intrigues were impelled by a commander from a state police agency who was determined to boost his own state career by unearthing and demonstrating that corruption seeped throughout the ranks of the Baltimore Police Department's command staff.

Tabeling got embroiled in the mess when one of his most trusted detectives was named as a party to the corruption. He returned from the National Academy to assist, and with his help, the detective, a man with an exemplary record of character and clearances, was exonerated in criminal court. But the sleaziness of the episode and the in-fighting it had incited left Tabeling feeling disillusioned. The work was demanding enough; obstacles to success were many, and recognition for exemplary performances were few.

In the end, politics dealt Baltimore yet another bad hand. Tabeling decided he had had enough as a detective. For the only time in his career, he asked the police commissioner for a transfer. Knowing that the Police Academy would benefit from a faculty member holding a master's degree, Pomerleau assented. Steve left his cherished detectives for a training and administrative post at the Police Academy.

CHAPTER

15

As he entered the Education and Training Division for his first day's assignment, Tabeling felt the butterflies, the first-day jitters. The new uniform he wore was unfamiliar apparel, but it felt good to be in uniform again after so many years. Now it was adorned by a gold lieutenant's badge, gold cuff braids, and commendations: eight bronze stars and forty-six commendation ribbons, tops in the department. The sight of such splendor merited a stir among the young recruits.

To step inside a classroom as the lecturer was a role Tabeling had never imagined himself filling. But over the span of his career, he'd found he had an affinity for explaining issues of the law, especially to skeptical detectives who felt put upon by what they viewed as lawyer's restrictions superimposed over their police prerogatives. Over the years, Steve had patiently explained, "No, not only does Miranda not impede us in our investigations, but it actually makes us better, more prepared investigators, able to get the relevant facts in a way that can be lawfully entered into testimony in a court of law." Similarly, Tabeling, who was facetiously known by his nickname, Get a Warrant, always advocated the many advantages of pursuing that early and vitally important step in any investigation.

He was bolstered in his belief. Without exception, the judiciary with whom he interacted lauded his attention to this most critical aspect of criminal investigation. Tabeling knew from experience that a warrant in hand precluded courtroom problems. Warrants helped to get convictions, period.

Very well then, he thought. *What better audience to impart these hard-learned principles than new officers.* They entered wide-eyed, just as he had done so many years ago, and they desperately needed to be thoroughly indoctrinated in the law. After all, they were to be its sole enforcers.

The Police Academy sat atop the department's new and modern eleven-story headquarters building, just east of the city's busy central business district. It featured a huge auditorium, a first-class crime laboratory, an enormous garage, a print shop, and a police academy that occupied the top two floors, replete with modern classrooms, conference centers, breakout rooms, and a modern, fully equipped courtroom for conducting simulated trials, the better to test young officers' capabilities to take the witness stand and to testify. There were physical training areas, a library, offices, and equipment rooms, together with a fully equipped weight room. It was a state-of-the-art facility.

Tabeling was conducted throughout the facility with staff members, and his spirits brightened considerably as he imagined the creative ways in which the courtroom could be used. Within an hour of unpacking and filling his new desk, he set to work, deciding which legal minds he had to enlist to make the testimony skill set most realistic for the student cops. He decided to ask Judge Robert Gerstung to participate. Well known by the cops of Central District where he reigned as the presiding judge, Gerstung delivered stinging rebukes to anyone in his courtroom guilty of intelligence lapses, cop or suspect. Though he liked and respected the police, he was quick to pull a reproachful trigger if he observed lazy or lackluster performance. Just as quickly, he charmed, joked, and traded banter when off the bench. But his strictness kept every officer, old as well as young, on their professional toes.

Tabeling also needed a state's attorney to try the moot cases, and he thought of no one but Howard Gersh, an attorney extraordinaire and a long-term fixture in the Homicide Division. A graduate engineer by education, he had choked when shown his new desk, enveloped as it was by seemingly hundreds of similar desks in an engineering boiler room, the nascent brain trust of a mega-corporation. Gersh instantly ditched the position and opted for law school, where, with his logical and creative brain, he excelled. Years later, he was trying murder cases in Baltimore, the murder capital, and as happy as a "sugarholic" in a candy factory.

Gerstung and Gersh—both esteemed names. The two men and their enormous store of practical experience were instantly outstanding contributors to the preparation and training of young police officers. Their inclusion as adjunct faculty members was an inspired choice.

Everything did not progress smoothly, however. Tenured law instructors, both holding law degrees, took umbrage at this upstart street cop arriving and making major changes to their hallowed way of doing things without even asking permission. Steve saw at once that although they both were law school educated, neither had passed the rigorous Maryland state bar examination. As he observed their teaching, he also noticed that their lectures included dated material that no longer reflected current conditions. Tabeling knew that the law was a living thing, constantly changing and demanding that its practitioners keep current. With Lexus Nexus, his expensive subscription service, he was assured of access to the most recent changes. Teaching outdated law procedures was like mastering the mechanics of a Model T. It had no place in the here and now.

So there were inevitable tiffs with the two incumbents, but Tabeling was determined to stand his ground. Eventually, the two shrugged their shoulders and acquiesced. There was a new sheriff in town.

Yet another cloud on the horizon appeared on Tabeling's day one. The academy director was a middle-aged retread from Chicago who had been recruited by the commissioner to take the training post.

He was, at best, a flawed authority figure who rarely was current with issues affecting staff, students, or curriculum. He prowled and poked his head into classrooms and offices alike. Tabeling thought the gestures were an attempt to show himself, for his patrols had no positive benefit. When other commanders told the director that Tabeling was "difficult to supervise," he saw fit to grade the new lieutenant's performance evaluation several levels lower than the man justly deserved. The poor rating was baseless and displayed a shallow character; the man held a position far out of his element.

Tabeling was never one to shrink from a conflict, especially when he was in the right, so he politely confronted the director. "By what right do you rate me this poorly? I've only talked to you once since I got here. Are you aware of the innovations I've instituted since then?" Tabeling enumerated enhancement over improvement, new development over badly needed remedial procedural rewrites, redesigns, policy changes to streamline duties, and improvements in maintenance and inspections. It was an impressive list, compiled in a short time.

The academy director shook his head. He chose not to dispute things he obviously knew little or nothing about, and he tore up the offending and inaccurate rating sheet and presented Steve with a new and much improved evaluation.

Tabeling warmed to the simulated courtrooms immediately, and he used his extensive practical knowledge, as well as cases culled from local publications and the subscription service he paid for—it published recent court cases, briefed and summarized for easy conversion into classroom presentations. The recruits responded favorably to the realistic training. It equipped them with skills that were essential after graduation. Tabeling meant to furnish the students with the knowledge he had never received during his academy days. Cases were developed in the classroom, from initial call to preliminary investigation, crime scene examination, evidence recovery and processing, witness location, interview, and statements taken. Then the investigation was summarized in the report-writing exercise. These documents were particularly valuable; they would serve as guidelines for criminal charges upon apprehension of the suspect(s), and they were invaluable aids to guiding testimony on the witness stand. They did more; they were the bases for crime analysis and were entered into databases that contributed to patrol allocation and related long-term studies. Finally, they were used to compile crime statistics for publication.

There was much more to the curriculum. Unlike any other bureau or division of the department, the Education and Training Division was audited every two years as to its adherence to state mandates regarding police training. The Training Commission mandated over five hundred training objectives that covered the complex functions and duties of a law enforcement officer in the state of Maryland. The auditors descended and asked academy staff to produce tangible proof that Recruit A, assigned to Class 75-4, received training objectives (usually selected randomly) numbers 12, 73, 213, 400, and 517. Once that was demonstrated to the auditors' satisfaction, staffers were asked to prove—via a visual inspection of the completed test papers—that the recruit had been tested on each of the objectives. If a question had been missed, staff then had to demonstrate that the recruit had been corrected and subsequently got it right. It was an enormous amount of recordkeeping, especially since the commission auditors might ask about a class that had graduated more than a year ago.

Failure to pass the audit assured very bad consequences, including decertification of the academy, a potential catastrophe for any police agency. Tabeling worked constantly to ensure that the performance—by instructors, administrators, and record keepers—conformed to state standards. It was ceaseless work.

He entered the classroom for the first time to instruct recruits in criminal law. With more than his share of practical knowledge, courtroom testimony, ceaseless study, and discussion with members of the Judiciary of Maryland, Tabeling was far better equipped than most instructors to impart meaningful perceptions and practical insights. His days also were filled with administrative and training duties, and he found himself quite gratified, if exhausted, by his efforts.

The recruits labored mightily. They were expected to master the elements of crime, report writing, patrol and investigative techniques, car stops, and vehicle operation—the final driving test to qualify for a departmental driving permit was a test from hell, replete with cones stacked on the passenger's side floor that were apt to topple if the vehicle skewed off vertical on a turn or jerked during a panic stop. The result would be failure of that part of the test and an immediate and apprehensive do-over. Additionally, the recruits had physical training, usually running three miles; self-defense; baton tactics; firearms range; and safe handling of the Smith & Wesson .38 special revolvers to attain proficiency, particularly about the circumstances guiding its use. They were tested weekly; two failures, and the recruit was dropped. The same result occurred for the second unexcused lateness. Lying, verbally or in writing, was an automatic ticket back to civilian status. Loud, abusive, profane behavior—terminated. Conduct reflecting discredit on the department— gone.

It was a very busy place, made more so by the fact that the Training Commission mandated annual in-service training for all veteran member sergeants and police officers. Thus, about three thousand members crowded the training facility in fifty-week cycles to be taught, tested, and receive recertification as police officers in the state of Maryland. Failure of that test could result in termination. As a courtesy, the department also trained officers from seventeen other agencies and occasionally conducted seminars over and above those that were mandated by the state. Over the course of a full year, over five thousand members received training at the Baltimore Police Academy.

It was a frenzied pace, and Tabeling reveled in it. He still was pursuing a higher degree and advanced certification at Loyola, so his days were a blur of activity, interaction, and consequential contribution. He richly enjoyed his new position, so different from anything he had ever known. But then, an opportunity from a totally unexpected source came calling.

CHAPTER

16

Tom Coppinger stood high on the list of highly respected commanders in the Baltimore Police Department for his perpetually calm demeanor and his soft-spoken ways. He was a man who treated everyone with respect. He held a law degree from the University of Baltimore and capably led the men and women of the Northern Police District, a fourteen-square-mile slice of the city that encompassed the poshest neighborhoods in town and the most depressed and every social strata between the two. He'd known Steve Tabeling for many years and had a healthy respect for his accomplishments as an investigator, as an innovative manager, and as a man. Tabeling was naturally curious when Coppinger asked him to meet.

"I've been contacted by people at Johns Hopkins Hospital on behalf of their security force," Coppinger confided. "Seems they want me to take over the director's position, overseeing all security operations on their downtown campus. It's a really big deal. My question to you is, would you be interested in going there with me as my assistant director? You'd have a lot of autonomy, and they could sure use your police sense and investigation capabilities. What do you think?"

For once, Tabeling was taken completely by surprise. The prospect took some serious consideration. To be sure, the offer was the highest compliment. Johns Hopkins, after all, was in a class by itself as a prestige hospital, one that drew patients from all over the nation and beyond. It was annually recognized as America's number-one hospital, a singular honor earned by its proficient medical staff, state-of-the-art facilities, and extremely high marks on its quality of care. The Johns Hopkins name was the gold standard for health care.

Just so, Tabeling considered that the facility occupied acreage in the Eastern District that abutted extremely challenged, violence-wracked neighborhoods, where gunshots often punctuated days and nights. Drug turf wars, carjackings, street robberies, and every manner of assault and battery marred the adjacent landscape. Like a war zone, the once elegant and gentrified Broadway now featured boarded three-story homes among the gorgeous housing, once occupied by Baltimore's elite families.

What Tabeling did not then know was that as prolific as pilferage and thievery occurred on the streets adjacent to the hospital's buildings, the same or more was taking place *inside* the institution. Upwards of thirty thousand people visited the hospital each day, in addition to its ten thousand employees, including an elite cast of physicians and technicians. The security staff, presently organized and staffed by a national security service, had proven itself unequal to the challenges. The hospital had decided to reach out and procure homegrown talent via the command staff of the Baltimore Police Department.

The very thought of making such a move both exhilarated and enervated Tabeling. On the one hand, the department, with all its deficiencies, was a thing he knew and that knew him. He knew its pitfalls, its heroes and villains, and its saving graces. It was a living thing to him and, all things considered, it had been very good to Stephen B. Tabeling. It had paid his bills, put food on his table, and underwritten the expenses of his education, which were still ongoing. It was, in its purest sense, a surrogate family, and he had grown very fond of it.

On the other hand, the opportunity to work for a prestigious institution like Johns Hopkins was nothing to take lightly. He knew instinctively that such an opportunity wouldn't come a second time. It was a ticket to another career and a passport to a new set of skills totally unrelated to police work, though oddly linked to them; skills of enormous future potential and value to him and to his family. Tom Coppinger's simply phrased question ended everything in Steve's current professional orbit. A new horizon was appearing, and he prayed he knew the right direction to track.

Honey and her thoughts came first. Together at their kitchen table, they hammered the pros and cons of the issue—pension from the police department, new salary, the hours that would be required, the quality of the people he would be tasked to supervise, the budgetary concerns, the responsibilities, the liabilities, the capabilities, and authority he would possess. Many more questions gushed like a waterfall, and the man and his beloved wife sat up past their bedtime thrashing them out and airing their concerns. It was really too much to simplify, for it was truly a matter beyond simplification.

The emotions the issue stirred, however, could not be quantified. From early adulthood, Steve had been a cop. A cop was *who he was*. It was his identity, and though he never crowed about his status among the top cops of Baltimore, his place had been earned and remained a constant source of quiet pride for him—and, truth to tell, for his bride as well.

For the last time in his career, he decided to turn to the one man who would advise him without any bias or bull: Donald Pomerleau. Though they'd had their share of disagreements, Tabeling appreciated that the commissioner was someone who knew him and his place in the department.

Pomerleau received him cordially enough and listened quietly as Steve explained the position and his new anticipated duties. The old man looked Tabeling in the eye and said without preamble, "I think you should take it."

With those few syllables, Steve was confident of the path he needed to tread. *Had the commissioner had something in mind for me,*

Steve reasoned, *now would have been the ideal time to say it.* By not saying it, the commissioner had said all that Steve needed to know. He thanked the commissioner, and they parted company.

Saying good-bye to colleagues of many years was the most difficult thing to do, made the more so because of the bonds that grow between cops, which few others understand—partners sharing boredom, risks, rainy days, futile stake-outs, and laughter. All those things were behind him. A major chapter of his life was closing.

He set his mind—thoughts, imagination, accumulated knowledge of the law and policies and procedures that might prove helpful in the months ahead—and prepared to make a transition he never expected he would make: to become a civilian security specialist in one of the most prestigious institutions in the world.

Decision made, now he entered the corporate world.

CHAPTER

T he first day of any venture is guaranteed to create memorable stress, and Tabeling's entry on duty at the Johns Hopkins downtown campus was no exception. He did well to mask his emotions behind his normally placid façade, but he was sorting out at high speed the people, processes, and pathways he needed to absorb. That the fifty-acre campus is a confusing labyrinth of juxtaposed buildings, old and new. Each serves specialized functions, and each is a warren of rushing human tides. Every person he passed seemed to need to be someplace else in a hurry. The current nationally known security force was not getting rave reviews from the guiding hands of the hospital, so they were on their way out. He noted with concern that all of the frenzied foot traffic that constantly flowed in and out of the buildings appeared to be completely unregulated; there were no security checkpoints. People moved wherever they pleased, without impediment, scrutiny, or notice. He thought, *There should be better control than this. Anybody could walk in here from the street. With anything.*

His first judgments were necessarily about people. He knew that no manager could be successful without good people—people on whom he could depend and trust. Starting any new job was hard enough, but not having trustworthy employees—employees he knew—meant progress would travel over far more demanding terrain.

The good news was that he knew dozens of men and women from the police department, many of whom were near or at retirement age, who might be interested in making the jump. He reached out, and the response was gratifying. Those he selected manifested not only good attitudes and hardy work ethics but skill sets that he reckoned would prove useful. One came from internal investigation, one was a traffic investigator, and some crackerjack investigators came from homicide. Still others had useful writing skills or were administrators, and all of them possessed a strong work ethic. He meant to build a team of interdependent people and skill sets, so he could rely on their accumulated expertise in times of need.

Then Tom Coppinger contacted him. Things had come up, it seemed, and he would not be taking the director's job at Johns Hopkins after all. Tabeling was thunderstruck. He had always been a man who liked to plan his moves with minimal variables to worry about. Now the linchpin of the program would not be arriving. Without too much drama, the hospital named Steve the interim director, and the frenetic pace continued unabated.

As he'd planned, he continually walked every corridor and hallway in every building, noting curiosities, concerns, bottlenecks, pedestrian traffic jams, and crowded entryways. Only infrequently did he see security members, and sometimes they were clustered, chatting, or enjoying the view, like tourists. When he inquired, he was informed that the security employees had no post assignments, simply because regular patrol areas did not exist and never had. He was appalled at this. It was a chaotic approach to attaining a level of coverage to ensure safety and equally accessible security officers to prevent or deal with a crisis. This was not management; it was anarchy, and he wondered why it had not been addressed earlier. Then he realized that he was here precisely because the powers that be had had enough of such slapdash security.

Maps of the hospital grounds and building interiors existed and were procured, and the scrutiny began. With accurate figures regarding security guard strength on each shift, tentative post boundaries were sketched, and guidelines were drafted for the optimum performance expected. Numbers of patients per hour could be plotted or at least estimated, and some basis for workload comparisons were established. Past issues—at least those few that had been documented—might also be helpful. Sometimes past trouble areas were predictive of potential future issues. Hours of shifts were regularized; a relief factor was calculated; supervisory spans of control and responsibilities were created. The responsibilities went on around the clock, and that was a work environment Steve understood only too well from his days and nights in the police department.

The Johns Hopkins campus was a bustling village in the heart of Baltimore; it was a magnet to multitudes of patients and sufferers, and it was a shining bright light of hope to thousands of others who one day would desperately need its world-class professional services and care. As such, it had to be kept safe, for it simply would not do to allow such a paragon of assistance and caring to be plagued by thieves, thugs, or worse.

Slowly, the magnitude of what he had signed on to do began to seep into Steve's consciousness. Possibly for the first time in his adult life, he felt the slightest tremor of doubt about his abilities to orchestrate the great array of human and material resources the job entailed: to gather and organize and coordinate them; to command and control them, and, most importantly, to adequately communicate his vision and further advance his mission to preserve and protect this precious island of healing and health.

Fortunately, the art and science of organization came naturally to him, from the days of helping his father in the basements of old rowhouses to leading a squad of police officers deployed across a police district. He felt justified in his successes. He felt as well that most police he had led responded well to his direction because, whenever possible, he explained the reasoning behind the decisions. And most people responded well to being let in on how the decisions affecting them got made. So it would be here. To the men and women who followed him from the police department, Steve Tabeling was already a known entity—a steady, calm, rational man who made rational decisions; a man who would listen to the occasional improvement to the plan and, if it had merit, implement it; a man people could talk to and reason with.

The organizational phase, once planted in good soil, would germinate and thrive. But there were more considerations. So many, many more.

As posts were established to cover the entire campus, the officers reported observing a few hospital employees who appeared to be part of the problem, for example, of things disappearing. Employee pilferage was hardly a new development in the security world, but the substances, chemicals, and drugs, including narcotics, stored throughout the hospital, sometimes with less than stellar security measures, added another level of complexity to the equation.

Compounding operational issues was the fact that the officers had never been adequately trained in arrest procedures or given training in self-defense techniques or the essentials of handcuffing and transporting an arrestee. An officer ignorant of such fundamentals was a danger to the suspect, himself, and anyone in the vicinity of the apprehension. To compound the issue, communication was parlous between units and supervisors, which always was a cause for grief.

There was another less tangible issue, one rarely uttered and much less discussed. Most of Tabeling's employees, certainly those emigrating from the police department, were members of a generation that held certain unspoken but conventional views. One such view maintained that doctors were a sacrosanct subculture to which mere men and women deferred. If true, that meant that doctors could not be second-guessed, much less suspected of doing something unlawful. To the generation under Tabeling's direction, doctors were above reproach; they were untouchable. Yet they were human—all too human, as events would demonstrate—and just as subject to temptation as anybody else.

Frenetic vital campus, staffed by some of the finest medical talent on the earth, patients and family from all over the country and many foreign countries, languages as proliferate as the United Nations, ceaseless activity, pedestrian and vehicular traffic flow, constant deliveries and incessant new construction and daily medical crises where life itself swung by a filament and some tiny flawed image of the enormity of the place became perceptible and conceivable. It was a consummately unfathomable enterprise, something to be held in awe.

Operational realities trumped lofty comprehensions. People were always being human, no matter the loftiness of their stations or assignments. And people who looked to take advantage of their moments or opportunities might often become quite comfortable and possessive of them, seeking to return and do the thing they did again and again—to take something, for example, that was not theirs.

Tabeling charged his officers to be observant, to ask questions, and to notice things and hear things, like good cops do. Of course, the fact that they worked their professions on a prestige medical campus demanded certain adjustments to behavior, a certain etiquette, and a deference to all persons encountered. Like a big creature treading on eggshells, one should avoid giving offense at all times. Pleasantness must prevail. There should be amiable chats, not interviews or, heaven forbid, interrogatories. And under no circumstances (except quite dire ones) was a member to put his or her hands on someone, unless, of course, no conceivable other alternatives existed. For them to instill a sense of safety for self and subject *and* deference stretched credibility to its limit, but so it had to be in a prestige place like Johns Hopkins Hospital. The mandate was to safeguard all: people, place, and property, without stepping on *any* toes.

Tabeling was not surprised that crime gave zero deference to Johns Hopkins or its famous names. The exterior teemed with street crime. Opportunists, like most thieves, knew that much of the big buildings' clientele had money. The better to get some from their person at the end of a knife or out of their vehicles foolishly parked on Monument or McElderry Street or one of a dozen others in walking distance. People hated to pay parking fees, so many of them chanced it. Tabeling read the reports with growing frustration. He had neither the human or material resources nor the crime analysis resources to target likely places and times outside of the institution. What was needed there was beefed-up city police forces dedicated to pacifying the approaches in and off campus. He would address that later. For now, he turned his vision to the interior of the campus—all the many miles of corridors, offices, patients' rooms, operating rooms, lecture halls, cafeterias, lounges, and other myriad amenities, including the medical and nursing schools, that comprised the dynamic town that was the Johns Hopkins Hospital campus.

And like any busy concern, there were innumerable barely noticed recesses, archaic practices, and outdated or flawed procedures that could never be known to the new security director except by happenstance. People in the work environment evolved ways of doing things, often to save time, others merely to cut corners, or possibly because a better way had never been identified or implemented or enforced. Carelessness invariably crept into work patterns— sloppiness, indolence, less-than-stellar ways of doing things—as in any large and complex workplace.

Steve Tabeling was a product of a workplace that, though not without its faults, demanded accuracy, precision, and follow-through, since the work outputs, in many cases, were subject to judicial scrutiny, both in the criminal and civil courts. Prosecuting homicide cases demanded due diligence, dogged determination, and precise focus. Anything less invited failure.

The practice of medicine was quite similar. What differed between the two, Tabeling saw at once, was an occasional lack of systemic precision, where secondary matters were concerned: filing systems, drug security, patient confidentiality, and others. Merely discovering the deficiencies, though not strictly security matters, had the potential to find its way to his desk. Thus, though not his bailiwick, per se, it was his to ponder.

By the same token, it simply would not do to direct his officers to scan for problems like a police patrol officer would be expected to do, nor should they scrutinize internal procedures. Private security didn't work that way, and such actions would invite conflict. The inefficient way would be to wait until a complaint was made or an item was reported missing or a trespass committed—inefficient, to be sure, but far less likely to light fuses. Once the transgression or error came to light, however, then remedial measures could be formulated and recommended. It was an incremental way to solve problems, but for the early months on duty, he could see no other.

Most challenging was that the current security service had no formal reporting system, which vastly complicated the possibility of assessing the extent of illegitimate behavior and obfuscated other issues of legitimate workload. Without a formal reporting system, resource allocation would remain a crapshoot. Seeing this, Tabeling created a simplified report form geared to simplicity—essential when dealing with employees, some of whom were not confident readers or writers, to which Steve Tabeling could relate. As reports were taken and recovered by Tabeling's office, they were collated and sorted by shift and then by building, victim analysis, suspect information, elapsed time to handle the incident, and other, equally important management concerns. The solution did not come easily or quickly. Slowly, with fits and starts, workload profiles began to emerge—those areas that were more likely than others to generate security-related issues and hence need dedicated human resources.

But if he was concerned that the issues would not come to his attention, he needn't have been. Within a few weeks, he was inundated with issues that needed to be addressed and remediated. Food service cash receipts were returned in sealed envelopes, for example; increasingly, the money receipted and certified as present was missing when turned in to the office. Investigations disclosed an employee was dipping prior to delivery. The employee was charged criminally, and the problem abated.

The security officers were made aware that no lawful arrest could happen unless probable cause existed, just like in the world outside the hospital. They were expected to know that probable cause consisted of "facts and circumstances sufficient to convince a reasonable and prudent man in an instance under scrutiny that a crime had occurred and that the person in custody was the likely suspect." Nothing less sufficed, particularly when arrest was contemplated. The alternative was the real possibility of a lawsuit.

Reporting forms and a modicum of legal training was not a perfect equipage, but it had to suffice and was far better than what had been in place upon his arrival. It was only a start, however.

Meanwhile, issues didn't wait for the security force to attain peak proficiency.

In a bizarre manifestation of academic competition, security was notified that several important cancer research studies had been destroyed. Determining motivation was difficult to ascertain but led to suspects. Several students engaged in the same experiment were "handicapping" classmates in an effort to achieve primacy in experiment findings—and presumably higher grades. Competition between brilliant students went far beyond collegiate pranks. Unacceptably so.

The problem of disappearing narcotics was a rare but vexing situation. It was stopped after Tabeling acquired cameras, had them concealed in smoke detector cases, and hung them with vantage views of the cabinets being looted. Medical personnel were apprehended, and the stealing ceased. Just such an incident, judiciously leaked to other staffers, appeared to have a definite preventive effect. After all, who wanted to risk the disgrace of apprehension or termination? It became obvious there was a new sheriff in town, and to many, it was a thoroughly pleasing reality.

To combat the problem and prevent a recurrence, Tabeling's more tech-savvy members researched, acquired, and installed a card-reader system designed to record time of entry and exit for all personnel using access to the affected laboratories; similar systems were scrutinized and considered for other sensitive areas. As a solution, it was an incremental approach, but since the problem was in place upon his arrival, reaction was the only possible thing to do. He vowed to master proactive measures whenever potential issues could be anticipated and realistically addressed. As an example, to forestall incidents of harassment of employees or visitors on foot, an escort service was created. Inspection of all packages being brought into hospital facilities was also instituted; when challenged, Tabeling cited an earlier US Supreme Court decision that held that such a policy was a reasonable one and had upheld such a procedure.

The establishment of regular posts, with assignments of one officer for each shift, was a system constantly scrutinized and refined and did much to add to a feeling of safety within the hospital grounds.

Security officers were schooled and conditioned on the importance their demeanor played in creating an atmosphere of security. Their manner of addressing people, particularly if those people had recently been traumatized, was of paramount importance. The Golden Rule was liberally applied. Members were reminded that many, if not most, of the visitors were coming to see loved ones, some of whom were desperately ill, so they were to apply a healthy dose of empathy to their interactions.

Unfortunately, bolstering the physical safety of visitors, staff, and patients effectively ceased at the hospital's boundary. Though jurisdictions were concurrent, it was the responsibility of the Baltimore Police to patrol and secure city streets. Tabeling's force was not large enough and was not adequately trained or equipped to patrol city streets. To Steve, the logical solution was to petition the police department to bolster its presence around the Johns Hopkins complex. It was logical to the hospital, that is, but when the proposal was presented to the commissioner and his deputy commissioner, it was flatly rejected. That was a private organizational matter, it was reasoned.

Tabeling refused to let the matter go away. He petitioned the Johns Hopkins attorneys to enlist their support in creating persuasive arguments, something attorneys were very good at doing, and making a compelling plea to reconsider. Tabeling participated; he knew the department pretty well and knew what kind of issues resonated with it. More important, he knew the kinds of issues the city government might find compelling. Money was one. Manpower was another, as were employment issues—jobs were of paramount importance in a city where tens of thousands of residents were unemployed. And taxes, of course. As an entity, Johns Hopkins was a significant part of the Baltimore city landscape and future, not to mention being its largest employer. The factors added up to a significant stack of bargaining chips.

Tabeling reasoned that the police department refusal was based on simple logistics and politics, as well as fiscal concerns. They simply didn't have enough officers to allocate a sizeable force and dedicate its use to a private institution. He understood that such a practice would set the other major hospitals to clamoring for the same service. But he knew that the continued success of Johns Hopkins depended on their ability to provide a safe environment to the families who needed them, in and outside of the facility, as well as the employees.

Then he hit upon a solution, both simple and elegant. Hopkins had the need for additional police presence. And Johns Hopkins had the money, due to its status and remarkable success. Let the police department allow its officers to work overtime posts paid for by Johns Hopkins. Posts would be created by the hospital security staff and worked in an overtime capacity. Overtime was the bane of police commanders and elected officials because it cost so much; now the problem was solved to each party's satisfaction. And it would make the police officers delighted; extra money was always a pleasure to earn. And this would be easy money, patrolling busy streets on foot and making their presence known.

The plan was fleshed out, put in writing, and presented to the department, and in no time, it was approved. Analysts and managers who examined its provisions simply could find no downside. It proved an instant success, and the word quickly went out to east Baltimore thugs: rob somebody up the street from Johns Hopkins. The hospital campus was no longer the happy hunting grounds. Almost overnight, street robberies on the periphery of the hospital and larcenies from autos virtually ceased. As a creative solution to a difficult problem, it was a huge success—money gladly paid out and worth every penny.

CHAPTER

18

A year had passed in the flash of an eye, it seemed, with Tabeling growing more and more confident in his new role as civilian security director. Although there had been slips and miscues, most were the result of inexperience, and all became learning points, duly noted. But overall, his performance got very good reviews from his superiors and hospital personnel. People felt safer than they ever had, due to the efforts of the new, better-led, and better-trained security force.

Just as Steve felt he had achieved a level of competence and confidence, and he quietly reckoned that this would be the career that would lead him to retirement, he had an unexpected visitor from Maryland's Eastern Shore, an attorney named Ruark. He came representing his dad, the mayor of the city of Salisbury, a placid community and quaint way stop for many Marylanders on their annual treks to Ocean City. Mr. Ruark had an offer to make.

After first thanking Steve for taking the time to see him, he got immediately to the point. "My father, the mayor, has followed your career here at Johns Hopkins with interest for some time," he said. "As you probably know, Salisbury is a growing city, and in many ways it's gaining big-city problems along with its growth."

He mentioned crime as a burgeoning problem; Eastern shore people were not used to that, nor were they comfortable about letting it continue if they could do something about it. "Something proactive," he said. "The mayor asked me to approach you with an offer, Mr. Tabeling. We're asking you to consider becoming Salisbury's new police chief."

Tabeling was taken totally by surprise. It was unheard of, not to mention quite flattering, but something so far out of his conscious thought that he hardly knew how to respond. With his head in a whirl, his thoughts jetted from the logistics, the need to relocate, dragging Honey halfway across the state—the list of considerations seemed endless. Then there was the real consideration of leaving behind all he had formulated at Johns Hopkins, just as it had begun to gel.

"I hardly know what to say," Steve responded.

Mr. Ruark held his hand up, palm outward. "I completely understand your feelings. We expected it to be a difficult decision for you, and we are prepared to wait while you take the time, gather your thoughts, discuss it with your family, and then decide." He went on to discuss the salary and benefits, which were generous and a significant advancement to his present financial status. They included a department-furnished vehicle, liberal leave, and substantial health and retirement benefits. Steve thanked the man profusely and told him that he would give the matter serious consideration and contact him as soon as possible. Steve's next order of business was with his loving wife.

Honey's reaction to the offer was astonishment. She wasn't quite certain where Salisbury was located, so Steve showed her a map. Honey's face hardly glowed with satisfaction. She was as proud as ever of her husband, but she nevertheless had grave misgivings. Even though the children were all grown and on their own, leaving their home and all they had known their entire married lives was a bit much. She listened but slowly shook her head. "I don't know, Steve. I never planned on anything like this. And so far away. When will we ever see the kids?"

Steve was prepared, and he too was caught between feelings of elation and doubt. Deep down, however, he knew he had to try this. Deep down, he had always wanted to be a police chief, someone with the power to make decisions about tactics, deployments, investigations, personnel, and dozens of other things. He wouldn't have to look over his shoulder at a half dozen bosses, all lined up to second-guess his decisions; there'd be no more abuse from superiors intoxicated with power. He'd truly be his own man; he could do good work and feel good about doing it. It was a dream come true.

"Honey," he said softly, "I need us to work together on this. At this stage, there's no assurance I'll even get the job. I'll need to have interviews before the town council—a number of them—so they can decide if they like me. Anything could happen. Then there's the mayor. I have to impress him as well." He paused, letting everything sink in, while she considered the unaccustomed serious expression on his face. "What do you say? Let's hear what they have to say? Can't hurt, right? Then if we decide it's not for us, we can go on about our lives like nothing ever happened. Okay?"

She was not sold, not a bit, but she nodded her head. To make her husband happy, she would have done anything. "Go on, if you want, Steve. See where it takes us," she said, but in her heart, she was wondering how she would ever break the news to their children that Mom and Dad were moving God-knew-where.

The decision was easier for Tabeling. He contacted the Salisbury mayor and indicated his interest in the position. In short time, he was before the Salisbury Town Council, an austere but not unfriendly gathering of local men who did politics in their spare time.

"Tell us," one intoned, "why you feel qualified to come to our town and take over the police department as our chief?" He held up his hand. "We all understand you are a big-city cop, now a security director and all, and that's all good, but how does any of that translate to us here on the Shore? We are different people down here, you know."

Tabeling composed his thoughts for a moment and then modulated his voice, as he often did when testifying. "First of all, I want to thank you all for inviting me here. It's very gratifying and flattering, and I am pleased to have been invited. I think my knowledge of policing in Baltimore City is a plus to the City of Salisbury. I have gained insight to problem solving and management techniques. I have had experience as a commander of a very successful narcotics unit. As a Lieutenant in the Homicide Division, I have handled many high- profile cases. I have experienced all facets of policing, from a street patrol officer to an Assistant Commander of Education. My experience at Johns Hopkins Hospital enhanced my management skills. I believe these skills will elevate my capabilities as Chief of Police in Salisbury."

"Director Tabeling, what makes you want to leave such an important position at such a place to contend with being the new chief of the Salisbury Police Department?"

It was a fair question, one that had no doubt crossed more than a few minds. "Why leave a prestigious place with a good salary in your own hometown to relocate down here to work for us?"

Though it was a question he hadn't anticipated it, he fielded it with composure. "Part of the reason I am interested in the position involves the important fact that for most of my career within the Baltimore Police Department, I aspired to be a chief someday. As you work in a big organization like that, you get to see how things get done, how decisions get made, and so on, and you naturally think you'd like the opportunity to be the one making the decisions, if you see what I mean—the man in charge."

It was a forthright answer, honestly expressed since it was totally true.

The questions continued, mostly in a neighborly vein. No one went for the jugular, just citizen councilmen being very careful about who they were to choose for their town's top law enforcer. And they were nothing if not thorough. The questions ran the gamut of organizational queries, missing little in their search for the perfect candidate. He was asked about personnel policies—what kind of people should get moved up in the department. What kinds of testing should be implemented, and who should grade, administer, and process the results? What was his position on constitutional rights? On Miranda rights, for example? Had he had run-ins with judges before? Had he lost cases because of improper procedures? The questions tumbled like an avalanche, threatening to bury him in rhetoric, yet Tabeling felt himself relaxing into the role of interviewee, and he began to enjoy the give-and-take. After several grueling hours for all of them, the members pronounced themselves sated—for now. They would take what he had said and ruminate on it and get back to him. Steve thanked them, shook hands all around, and took his leave. On the long drive home, it occurred to him that the Salisbury elected leadership certainly seemed to take their responsibilities seriously. *Not a bad thing*, he thought.

Seriously, indeed. He was summoned for two more similar grillings in the weeks ahead. It was obvious the officials didn't want to make a mistake and hire someone who did not have the knowledge and ability to lead the police department. This was the administration's first attempt to hire an outsider. They wanted to be sure they made the right choice. The third get-together was more of a walk-through, a last eyeballing, and a final get-to-know-each-and-all before offering him the job, which they presently did. He knew the major life adjustments that he and Honey would be called upon to make, relocation foremost and, strangely, the most difficult, as Honey was not warming to the prospect as he hoped she might. But she was ever the loving and supporting wife who had never stinted when her family needed her, least of all her Steve. She was not about to dig heels in now. She would do what he needed her to do and smile and try to adjust to it.

First he needed to inform the Hopkins Institution about his decision and then prepare his security staff for his departure. Both staff and administration expressed disappointment. They were regretful to a person, sorry to see a man leave who had accomplished so much toward making a safer work and healing environment in such a short time. He was thanked for the creative solutions he had implemented; for infusing his own enthusiasm for the work into most of his men and woman; and for opening the channels of communication between the administrators, medical staff, technical professionals, and his security personnel. It had been a rare and appreciated collaboration of ideas, cooperation, and mutual trust. He had raised people's opinion of the security force and the work it performed. He had made people feel safe again. And more than one bigwig intimated that the door would always be open to him, should he ever decide to return. It was a gratifying, poignant moment he would not soon forget.

They decided not to sell their house but to rent an apartment in their new town—another major concession by Honey and a huge adjustment for them both. Moving a lifetime's accumulation of furnishings, possessions, and Steve's professional journals, law books, and textbooks; making arrangements to continue his education; getting them safely established; and learning a town and its culture was totally foreign to them both. Honey needed to make friends and establish neighborhood relationships, while her husband needed to learn everything relevant to his new position in his new town.

Their first major lesson was not a pleasant one. They'd found a smart apartment, but it was located, they were told, in the county, a tongue of territory jutting between the city's irregular perimeter and thus not eligible for the chief's residence, More searching continued, and Honey decided to return to Baltimore while Steve took up a friend's kind offer to stay with his family during the real estate search.

In time, the mix-up got sorted out, and Tabeling could truly begin the complicated process of learning to be the best chief he could be. People, it was clearly obvious, were counting on him, big time.

His arrival and adjustment to the move was eased by the town's ebullient and personable mayor, who availed himself and his staff to aid Steve in the transition, going as far as to walk in the downtown business area, personally making introductions of his new chief.

Salisbury was an old town of sixteen thousand people, with factories, warehouses, and farms and numerous small enterprises. It boasted many houses of worship and a burgeoning financial center, serving the finance and business needs of much of the Delmarva Peninsula. Old towns tended to contain many old families, whose people had populated the place for many generations. Like any small community, most everybody knew or knew of just about everybody else, as well as about their business, most likely. People were cordial to the new chief and his wife but not overflowing with warmth. It was just cordiality, courtesy—the kind you show because you were raised right. After all, it wouldn't do to be cold to out-of-towners, especially when one of them was the new chief.

And Steve knew he had to proceed briskly but with caution. Just like his first weeks at Johns Hopkins, Steve dove in to learn the people, personalities, policies, procedures, and practices he needed to navigate in order to get the lay of the land and its politics. He learned who knew whom, who knew what, and who could be of immediate help in jump-starting the new chief's engine.

He soon was to realize that the learning curve for Salisbury and its mores and folkways, might be a tad steeper than any other he had scaled. He learned of relationships also—who was cousin to whom might have overwhelmed him, had he not decided to confine himself with the first level of consanguinity only. Salisbury was a Maryland community, to be sure, but it was its own unique place. Political alliances seemed a bit more convoluted to sort out and thus took patience, much listening, and study, not merely for his edification. Knowing who was likely to support whom was a survival skill of the first stripe in a closed community like Salisbury, where everybody went way back with so-and-so and political alliances were often difficult to sort out. Just as well, it was a road map to eventual success.

During his introductory interviews with the town council, some of the members had gone out of their way to express their concerns and deficiencies they had observed about the local police officers, issues they believed had serious potential ramifications.

"They are in trouble," voiced some of the members, referring to the local officers. "They know nothing about legal searches, and warrant writing does not come to them." Tabeling reassured them he was a staunch and experienced practitioner of the science of search-and-seizure writing, having been personally tutored by storied members of the Baltimore and state of Maryland judiciary.

He was as forthright about promotions, when asked, declaring that his preference for advancing members to supervisory positions included his assurance of their high integrity, not only in their professional lives but inclusively and that their decision-making and personal and professional dealings reflect honesty. "It is not easy to measure that quality," he had told them, speaking from experience. "But it is essential to make the effort. We must ensure that the candidate for advancement exemplifies all that a police officer must be—a model of truth. Nothing less is acceptable."

He assured the members as well of his staunch intention to thoroughly learn the community and the police department so as to accurately assess the needs of both—the specific requisites so as to assess what enhancements to initiate.

Learning departmental procedures naturally came easier; it was police work, after all, and a remarkably simplified version of policy and practices at that. The politicians had indicated during the interviews that the officers had experienced snags in a number of police practices; the handling of informants was a huge one. Reporting crimes sometimes did not get done in the timeliest manner, which slowed agency reporting to the FBI. Their Uniform Crime Reports emanated from most law enforcement agencies in the country through voluntary and timely compliance. UCR was the basis for national crime statistics and so was deemed vital to its numerous users. One solitary Salisbury employee, Tabeling learned, handled all the UCR reporting. After his compilation, the initial reports went to the Maryland State Police for preliminary assessment before forwarding to the Bureau. Tabeling early on got rumblings that the Maryland State Police were not thrilled by the timeliness issues of the UCR reporting from Salisbury PD or, in some cases, its veracity. He sensed a shiver down his spine at the thought of a dust-up with the Maryland State Police, especially at the outset of his career. That matter, he knew, had to be addressed immediately. It touched upon the department's integrity.

In line with that he turned much of his initial attention to the revamping of the crime report formats. No report form is more accurate than the officer doing the preliminary investigation and then completing the report, and an investigation is only as good as the officer's understanding of the elements of the crimes being reported, so a healthy and intensive course of instruction and training was called for immediately. Meanwhile, every report written reflected the state of each officer's *individual* comprehension of the reported crime, the elements that comprise that crime, and his or her ability to gather those facts and accurately record and report them.

The crime elements were fundamental to police reporting, but Tabeling had observed vast dissimilarities among the hundreds of police officers with whom he had worked in Baltimore. And even when all performed from the same sheet of music, individual supervisors were sometimes not above fine-tuning the notes to reflect local directions on the part of shift commanders looking to diminish the numbers. Steve was not sure but knew that much of the latter might well be the case in his new jurisdiction. Very definitively, the officers had to hear from the new top cop that accuracy, not low box scores, was the aiming point from this day on in the Salisbury PD and that he would back them on the issue—accuracy over crime decreases.

Truly there was much to do and the enormity and complexity of what confronted him nearly made his head swim. But he had signed on for this, and he meant to do his best for these people and fulfill their trust in him. It was his way to find and seek out improvements to the ways of doing things. It was what he did and what made him a success at each stop. So, while Honey decorated their new living place, Steve dove into the deep end.

CHAPTER

19

T he new position soon was every bit as complex as he thought it
might be. Procedures were one thing; they could be chiseled into
old granite and displayed prominently. But that meant nothing
if this person or that supervisor didn't agree and chose to ignore it.

Tabeling had been around long enough to understand that there
were official positions and then there were the way things actually
were. Like organizational charts, it usually was a waste of paper. The
organization that mattered, Tabeling knew, was the way people chose
to organize themselves. The informal organization actually reflected
reality; likes often congregated around likes. Weak players often
gravitated around stronger team members for support, protection,
and influence—or just to be seen with the stars. There were family
links, fraternal associations, political bonds. Then there were the
converse: feuds, grievances for another person that were nurtured
and allowed to fester; vengeance plotted and planned. There were
people who just didn't care for one another because he wronged my
cousin, disrespected my sister, snubbed me. People just didn't like
each other; organizational chart be damned.

The trick for any leader was not to diagram the affections and
antipathies, he knew. Nor was it to harness the energy intrinsic to

both volatile emotions. It was to get everybody pulling in the same direction, which meant the direction that the chief of police had reckoned. In short, he needed to define his objectives in clear, concise language and communicate his expectations to the troops—and then lead the way. And the sooner the better.

He also realized that any collection of people grouped together in a social system usually assembled themselves into a de facto social order: alpha males and females at the dominant or top end and more submissive (or merely cooperative) members at the opposite. Such social groupings did not take place overnight or without trauma; usually much psychological (and occasional physical) elbowing, contention and friction formed it, and the order emerged. From time to time, its stability might be upset by a disagreement or flare-up of old grievances, but an effective leader demonstrated his management acumen in controlling such scuffles and returning things to normal as soon as possible. A good leader kept the contentious people in hand and motivated. And working.

The arrival of any new member, however—especially one in a leadership role—threatened the stability of the balance of power and might well upset an alliance otherwise working in harmony. Or the new arrival might just tip other leadership individuals out of their orbit.

Shortly after his arrival, Tabeling received a call from the mayor, his new boss. "Chief, what's going on at the sight of that house fire?" the mayor asked. "I'm getting calls from all over the place. They're telling me it's a firebombing. You got anything on that?"

Tabeling felt himself in the crosshairs of the worst of dilemmas for a new appointee. Queried by his new boss about an important matter, he simply didn't have an answer. He confessed his ignorance. "Mayor, no one's notified me about that. Give me a few minutes and I'll have you up-to-date."

As fast as he could get to the police station, he found himself face-to-face with the daytime shift commander, an old line lieutenant who had sent negative glances Steve's way from their first meeting.

Tabeling wasted no time in getting to the center of the issue. "What's this about a firebombed house, Lieutenant? Are you aware of this?"

"We're on top of the matter, Chief," the man assured him. "I just sent word to the mayor, and—"

"Number one," Tabeling interrupted, fighting to control his temper, "you do not send *anything* to the mayor without my knowledge—not *ever*. Is that clear? Number two—"

"No, Chief, it doesn't work like that. You see, that's not the way we do things here. Here, I notify the mayor before anyone else," he said rather smugly. "Yeah, here we—"

"You're not listening to me, Lieutenant. I'm telling you *my* policy. And *my* policy says you notify me whenever anything of this magnitude happens. Is that *clear*?"

Inconceivably, it was manifestly not clear to the lieutenant, who stood before his new chief, shaking his head from side to side and scowling. "No, sir," he replied. "You see, down here, we—"

"Let me put this another way," Tabeling said clearly and calmly, after he had controlled his emotions. "Perhaps a way you'll better understand. When I give you an order, I expect you to carry it out, immediately and to the best of your ability. Is *that* clear?"

This last was met with the same apparent intransigence—body language that virtually bawled, *You're not the boss of anybody, Mr. Baltimore!*

Steve had had enough. Never on his worst days with the department had he ever observed such flagrant insubordination. This man needed to be taught a lesson. He could submit him to a formal discipline process, but that would be a poor start to his new career. Another tack was called for.

"Okay," Tabeling said calmly, "let's do this, then. Effective immediately, you are the new permanent midnight shift commander. Oh, and with permanent Tuesdays and Thursdays off. That's effective tomorrow night. Anything else? Good. Dismissed!"

The man stood before him, trembling with anger, his face glowing purple with each breath. "Oh, no, mister. You are not doing this to me. Do you know the people I know?" he raged. "You are not doing this *to me!*"

"I have already done it. The order will be in writing by the close of the workday. Dismissed!"

Unfortunate start though it was, the word about the senior lieutenant, regarded as quite a connected local, traveled throughout the land. *This new guy is for real,* it said. Not a great beginning but not altogether ineffectual. There were back-fills Steve was forced to make with friends of the new permanent midnight commander, but simple explanation of the discipline requirements of a modern police department clarified and sustained the chief and his actions. Deal done. He first turned his attention to the firebombed house, established that it was indeed a malicious arson, made good contact with the local FBI, and moved toward the clearance of the case in sprint time.

Not a bad first week, he thought.

Satisfactory to date or not, the more Chief Tabeling surveyed his new community, the more distraught he became. Little he saw or heard conformed to those things he knew to be accepted modern law enforcement practice. The Salisbury Department had seven officers who specialized in traffic enforcement. Why them? Simply *because.*

Tabeling had come from the largest department in the state, where the police commissioner, quite rightly, expected all of his officers to engage in traffic enforcement as well as in narcotics enforcement and crime suppression and directed patrol and the myriad other generalist functions that made them well-rounded cops and the most useful members of the law enforcement community. Early on, he saw that intensive training was going to be a number-one priority of his administration, and as he got to know his supervisory and command members, he also realized that, with few exceptions, the trainer was going to be *him.* He was fine with that. That way, they would hear it from his mouth, leaving zero room for misunderstandings.

He spent time each day in his police vehicle, often with an experienced member taking the tour. He grew intimately familiar with the town, its charm, topography, and anomalies but mostly its people. With a population over sixteen thousand, plus many more who came each day to work in the town, it was simply a good place to be. It was a healthy population with near full employment, nestled in just under fourteen square miles. He spoke with business owners throughout and downtown and listened to their aspirations and requests. Like business owners most everywhere, they wanted police officers assigned to foot patrol, the better to make their patrons and customers feel safe. With only seventy-five officers of all ranks, that was going to be a tough proposition, but he would do what he could.

Driving through the industrial section of the town, he was struck by the large numbers of vacant plants and warehouses, dormant areas that needed minimum presence of police. Duly noted. He met neighbors, spoke to the religious leaders, Kiwanis, VFW, and many other civic and fraternal groups. And the impression he created was increasingly favorable. Not only was the new chief neighborly, but he was experienced. Maybe that big city had taught him a lot about policing. And he seemed to know that Salisbury was definitely not the big city. It was Salisbury, and its people and ways of doing things were its and its alone.

He paid particular attention to the patrol posts or areas—their shape, juxtaposition, and size. He knew that patrol workload caused the area post to be reflective. High workloads—calls for service, for example—produced a *smaller post* vis-à-vis lower workload post sizes. Small posts reflected much more intense activity. But here, when he scrutinized the workload numbers—at least those he could locate—he found that sometimes the opposite was the norm. That was contrary to everything he had learned about workload analysis and patrol allocation. He knew a lot because he'd taken the time to attend seminars on the subject and read everything about it he could find. Intelligent deployments based on calls for service analysis was an essential platform for the efficient delivery of police services. Anywhere. The size and shapes of the posts, as he studied them and upon inquiries, appeared to be the result of incremental decision making on an ad hoc basis—someone who was chums with a council person, for example, or a previous mayor. In fact, no one could give Steve any comprehensive reasoning for the post shapes and sizes as they currently existed. Such a morass created disparate workloads, requiring some officers to run nonstop from shift start to finish, while others had few or no calls during their entire tour. It created potentially dangerous gaps in coverage and delivered wildly divergent police services to the residents, business owners, and visitors to their town.

There were more issues. He discovered that evidence was not stored in a secure facility to ensure the chain of processing prescribed by procedure and law; rather, evidence for a particular case might be stored anywhere—the trunk of a police car; a cop's garage; in a police locker. Such slapdash procedures violated the rules of evidence, where a chain of custody must be strictly adhered to overcome charges of evidence tampering that would render the object tainted and unfit for presentation in a court of law. It was Law Enforcement 101. It was yet another example of policy that needed to be made *now* with connected procedures hammered out, sent out, and enforced and strictly adhered to.

When reviewing the all-important budgetary documents, Tabeling instantly noticed a startling fact: Salisbury PD patrol vehicles were traded in every twelve months. Worse, the trade-in allowance averaged six hundred dollars on a ten-thousand-dollar vehicle, sometimes with as few as thirty-five thousand miles. This was a money hemorrhage that needed to be stopped.

Despite these and some other shortcomings, made more from ignorance of proper police procedures than any other reason, Tabeling was impressed with the officers themselves. He didn't hesitate to solicit their thoughts on policies, procedures, equipment, and the like, and they were not the least shy about sharing their thoughts. He found them to be an intelligent group of men and women who were eager to learn and improve themselves and their performances. And that discovery was a highly gratifying one because a police department cannot hope to be better than the people who comprise it. They were the foundation of the police department, and Steve sensed instantly that the foundation was a solid one.

One officer's complaints, however, troubled him. "Chief," the man said, "you need to know that this communications system we got is a problem." The other officers nodded their assent. "A fellow can be in trouble and asking for help, and you know what? Nobody can hear him. Don't know if it's the folds of the ground or the woods line or buildings or whatever. But you flat can't get out with these walkies."

Tabeling listened to the issues and promised to get things fixed as soon as he possibly could. When their impromptu meeting broke up, and the officers filed out of the roll call room, he wondered just how he was going to get the resources to do that.

CHAPTER

20

A tour of the communications facility confirmed the officers' complaints. It was efficient enough as to the people staffing it, but it was very old. Issues in safe dispatching and instantaneous transmission of communications are a critical factor in officer safety. It was yet another matter that needed to be addressed now. Tabeling knew that time was the most critical matter in all the issues confronting him, and innovative solutions had to be found and quickly enacted. The problem of money was a primary stumbling block. It simply would not do to hit town and then be seen as shaking down the town fathers and mothers. He was therefore strongly motivated to formulate a plan that might expedite and smooth his path. After conferring with all affected parties, including equipment providers, and then gathering his thoughts into strategy and his facts into a comprehensive plan, he asked to do a presentation before the town council.

"Gentlemen," he began, "as you know, I've spent these past weeks surveying our town and meeting its good people. And I'm pleased to tell you that it is every bit the beautiful place to live and work I hoped it would be." He paused for a second before continuing. "But that is not to say some things could not stand some improvement. And a few things critically need addressing as soon as possible. I view these latter as very serious matters affecting citizen and officer safety."

This caused a stir among the gathered officials. He held his hand up as a gesture of reassurance.

"What I am proposing today is the building and equipping of a new communication center." At their murmurs, he paused and then went on. "And I'm here to tell you that it will not cost the city of Salisbury a cent. We can build and equip that center just by reorganizing the monies we have right now, simply by being more efficient about how we allocate them.

"I can make this claim because I have taken the time to study the department's budget. Very interesting document. I've provided each of you with a copy of the current fiscal year's operating budget. If you'll turn to page fifteen, subtitled 'Vehicle Acquisition and Maintenance,' lines thirteen to twenty-four. According to this—and I've checked; it is an accurate accounting—departmental vehicles—there are seventeen, plus the chief's vehicle—are traded in after a mere twelve months' service. Of course, where I came from there was a huge disparity with such a policy as this, but that's probably not a fair comparison. Therefore, I ask that you look at this as consumers or car owners. Would any of you think it makes sense to get rid of a vehicle that's only one year old? Why, the engine's just broken in by then. And look at the low—I mean, relatively low—mileages on those vehicles! But that's not what truly concerns me. If you read down to line twenty-three, you can see that the average trade-in valuation afforded to us for buying new cars is only six hundred dollars." He paused to let that sink in and then continued.

"If I've done my math right, we are losing several thousand dollars per vehicle in value each time we do this. Now, if we use the vehicles for three years each, that will free up enough money the first year to build and completely equip a state-of-the art communications center, second to none on the Shore, and can then stop worrying if someone is going to get hurt because his call for a backup can't be heard. And since this is a safety concern of the first magnitude, I'm respectfully proposing you consider it immediately, tonight."

The officials seemed impressed and set in immediately to study the figures. The measure was authorized and endorsed. With remarkably little hassle, Salisbury would have a spanking-new communications center.

But Tabeling was not yet done. Indicating another page of the document before them, he demonstrated that another significant portion of the police department budget was being siphoned, so to speak, for gasoline for the use of the city's Department of Public Works vehicles. Obviously displeased at that news, the members vociferously vowed then and there to put that practice to a stop. So, in one meeting, two significant revenue drains were plugged.

After the meeting, he went on to inform the mayor privately that he intended to begin extensive training, department-wide, on report writing and on the FBI's Uniform Crime Reporting system, so that everyone would adhere to a consistent standard of performance. This information was imparted with a cautionary: Adherence to more accurate standards would undoubtedly result in rising crime rates, not because there was more crime but simply because crime was being reported *accurately*, maybe for the first time. But that would undoubtedly generate some political heat. His suggestion was to inform the public, and tell them that the first year would be the base year for the new system; the year against which subsequent years would be measured. Donald Pomerleau had done the same thing in Baltimore in the seventies. The base year was a bear and caused a stir in the press, but each succeeding year was lower and thus showed improvement. Continuing improvement, no less. It was a sharp move, and it restored the integrity of the system: a classic win/win.

The training began within the week. He observed that the qualities he had sensed in his officers, most of them, included a genuine desire to learn and to get better. It was gratifying to watch, and after a time, they seemed like sponges, insatiable when it came to learning new skills. Since he conducted much of the training, he came to realize that he was a born educator, and the irony amused him.

The days, and nights of labor exhilarated him like little he had ever undertaken. Time hurtled forward from month to month, but much was accomplished. At home, however, not all was tranquil. His wife, normally the most placid and loving of women, appeared increasingly distraught. Part of her despondency grew out of Steve's necessarily long hours away from her. But like anyone uprooted from her home and moved so many miles from her children and grandchildren, Honey pined for them, understandably so. It was not simply a matter of pacifying her. Inside she was grieving, like someone who had lost a loved one. It concerned him deeply, and he was destitute of ideas to reverse her mood and restore her happy nature. The more time elapsed, the grayer grew her temperament.

He resolved to do whatever it took to cheer her up, and in their free time together, he feted her with restaurants and long walks. The people they encountered were cordial to the police chief, less so to his wife, it seemed, and it pained him to see it. It was subtle, but he saw the pain in her eyes. And that was a sight he could not bear to see. Something would have to be done, and he pondered the matter incessantly.

Meantime, no rest for the energetic new chief. One night following a council meeting, as they filed out of the town hall, a call was broadcast over his police radio, advising that an armed holdup of the liquor store on Route 13 had just occurred. Wanted in connection were two white males, mid-twenties, both armed with handguns, and driving a tan sedan with damage to its rear end. It was last seen traveling at a high rate of speed, north on Route 13. Steve knew the store location and turned his vehicle around and sped off. With lights and siren activated, within a few minutes he saw, dimly in the half light, what appeared to be a light tan sedan traveling at high speed and erratically weaving between other vehicles. He accelerated and got on the radio, advising units of his position and requesting some to respond. Within a few minutes, he was gratified to hear the sirens of his officers as they approached from behind him. Accelerating a bit more, he got very near the suspect vehicle, close enough to observe that there were two men inside. The driver looked over at him nervously and attempted to accelerate as Tabeling pulled abreast of him and then passed him slightly and began to edge the suspect's vehicle toward the right shoulder. By alternately pulling ahead and then steering toward the suspects and then slowing, he was able, with the help of his swarming officers, to virtually surround and stop the tan car.

The men were ordered to exit with hands out in front of them. Then they were pulled to the pavement, frisked, and handcuffed. The swiftness of the capture and apprehension were a testament to the stellar teamwork of his officers. Once the prisoners were patted down and thoroughly secured, the trunk of the vehicle was popped, while officers also searched the car interior.

Steve observed two handguns in the trunk, as well as a bag containing various denominations of cash and masks. As one of his eager officers reached in to extract the evidence, Tabeling stopped him. "No," he said evenly. "There's a way to do this. We're going to get a search-and-seizure warrant. Remember what I taught you? We're going to do this right. Yes, we'll tow the car, and when we get it to the impound lot, and the warrant is signed and in our hands, *then* we search."

The young officers, awash in adrenaline, were visibly disappointed to hear this, but each calmed himself and did his part to carry out the chief's commands. Hearts pumping with excitement, they made a small procession to their evidence control section and awaited the signed warrant.

It arrived within thirty minutes, and again the trunk lid was popped open, and as they'd observed, there were obvious tools of the crime and its fruits in the vehicle's trunk. As Tabeling and the officer examined the interior, they noticed a newspaper from a North Carolina town. Its lead story featured lines about a recent jewelry store holdup and included the fact that two men were suspects. To his officers' astonishment, the chief indicated that a second warrant had to be written and signed. Another thirty minutes elapsed, and upon its arrival, the trunk was opened and the newspaper examined. Fascinated, Steve instructed all to stand by and called the North Carolina State Police, informing them of the arrests and the unfolding developments. They furnished him with priceless information on the suspects—the men were soldiers from Fort Bragg and were wanted in connection with a number of felonies in that state.

Once in legal possession of the paper, their eyes focused on the dim trunk interior and on a US Army ordnance box, the kind used to contain and transport ammunition. Beyond the belief of the Salisbury officers, Tabeling again insisted that a third warrant be obtained. Inured to his ways by then, the officers submitted without a comment. When *that* document arrived, they opened the ordnance box and observed it to be US Army property and filled with ammunition. After this discovery, the FBI was immediately notified and in due course appeared and took the two soldiers into custody.

Months later, a letter arrived from a federal judge, graciously praising the work of the Salisbury Police Department officers, especially their commendable foresight in obtaining not one but three search-and-seizure warrants for the same car in the same case. The judge went on to say that that intelligent precaution had made the case a very easy one for the prosecuting US attorney to win in court. It also demonstrated the wisdom of Steve Tabeling's favorite precept, "Get a warrant!"

Within months of his arrival, the new chief had plugged every leak he'd found—a new and effective evidence retention policy was adopted, one that kept the chain of custody secured; the new communications center was up and running and would soon be designated as a foul-weather control center for the entire region; a new patrol allocation was instituted and resulted in vastly faster police response to emergency calls; and new police report forms and improved procedures were in effect, and though crime inched up, the public had accepted it as a necessary downside to truth in crime reporting—and that it actually tended to make them safer. Calls and crime trended up as well, usually an indication of enhanced citizen trust and confidence.

This invariably led to the fact that the chief was bound to ask for a very unpopular measure: more police officers.

His justifications were impeccable, including the officers he had assigned to the downtown business district on foot. This was a very popular move with the downtown business community. With the increasing call volume and the optimum and average workload needed to provide sufficient time for crime prevention and directed patrol, the city could be made immeasurably safer to both residents and tourists. The safer environment would be more attractive to Eastern Shore tourists as well. Tabeling presented the numbers in black-and-white and then backed up the proposal with a list of the positive benefits that would accrue. He was asking that the department gain thirty-five positions, a sizeable increase. Nothing of that would happen without tax increases, never a popular option. The saving grace was that Salisbury had the lowest property tax rate in the region, and the significant increase in human resources could happen for only a few percentage points of increase. Totally popular it was not, but after much discussion and debate, the measure passed. The new officers would be carefully selected and added in increments. It was a stunning achievement, and Steve felt highly gratified. His word had been heeded; wisely, he thought.

More officers were approved but nothing happens that doesn't affect related things. More officers were not going to be well accommodated in the dated and cramped police headquarters, an antique. Something new needed to be gotten, and time was not on their side. Remembering the derelict industrial buildings he has seen early in his tenure, he toured the area anew. Like a godsend, he found an abandoned property; it had once housed the city's recycling center. *Well,* he thought, *let's see if we can recycle you one more time.*

It took some arm-twisting this time, but after a bit, the money was found; an architect's feasibility and conception study was completed. The building was acquired for next to nothing, and construction was set to begin. When his plans became public, the local press mocked the concept as "the Eastern Shore Taj Mahal."

But things at home were progressively deteriorating. Always a happy and compatible couple from their first days together, virtually as children, Honey, never a complainer, expressed her feelings in a most poignant manner to her husband. She, who had always put herself second to her family, could abide the situation no longer.

As much as he loved his position and the capabilities he brought to it, he was forced to concede that his marriage was worth far more to him than his job. Honey was his life, and she must come first. Sorrowfully and after much anxiety, he broke the news to the mayor. He would be leaving Salisbury.

CHAPTER

21

The transition from dynamic police chief and the accompanying anxiety that came with their move took much adjustment by both Steve and Honey, mentally as well as physically, but the Tabelings were an adaptable couple, and their marriage was a durable one; both adjusted in record time. Honey was delighted to be back with her loved ones amid familiar surroundings. Steve worried about his next position, but his reputation was robust enough to garner near immediate offers, Johns Hopkins Hospital Security foremost. They had formed a new subsidiary corporation to handle the multitude of security and logistical functions essential to a complex medical facility, one that was experiencing unprecedented growth. Tabeling fit the new position well, and his employment anxiety vanished.

After some months passed, he was approached by other potential employers, people he had known and worked with over the years. The interest in him was flattering, none more so than an offer from Loyola College, a campus he knew intimately as its long-term student, both undergraduate and graduate. It was an idyllic tree-lined parcel of academia, nestled in North Baltimore and attended by the sons and daughters of many of the city's finest old families and more than a few children of working-class couples, determined to obtain the best education available to them. Loyola enjoyed a superior reputation as a first-rate learning center; a distinguished faculty, both cleric and laity; and a slower pace than the hustle of downtown Baltimore and Johns Hopkins hospital, respected institution though it was. Loyola was smaller, quieter, and every bit as intense.

He sat for an interview before three of the college academics whose concerns reflected the different perspectives of a learning center like Loyola, quite at odds with much of his recent work in law enforcement. Knowing a healthy dose of adaptation would be necessary for success in this new position, he began his adaptation immediately, at the interview. Thinking on his feet was a Tabeling hallmark, though not all the interviewers were won over. But he did well enough to get a second interview with the college president, Father Sellinger, who knew him well enough to appreciate the huge upside Tabeling's presence would prove to the school.

Most understood that the security department was in need of rebuild. It was frankly in disarray. Father Joseph A. Sellinger, SJ, called on Steve Tabeling, whom he knew to be an able, intelligent, and perceptive man. The cleric responsible for providing executive leadership on the Loyola community campus was a sagacious man and a gifted judge of talent. He also knew Tabeling's reputation from his former employments and recognized as well that he was acquiring a dynamo, which the moribund security department needed. Easy to talk to but exacting, Father Sellinger was determined to catapult Loyola College to the ultimate of its potential, achieving estimable status, a tangible achievement that would one day result in its elevation to the level of a major university. Father Sellinger offered Steve Tabeling the job as Loyola College's Director of Security. Steve promptly accepted. It began a productive decade together.

As with any new venture, there was much to be done. Tabeling surveyed the organization and saw at once that there were no regularly assigned areas of responsibility for the security employees. They were aimless, responding to requests willy-nilly and making inadequate or no reporting of the incident subsequently. One of the biggest issues was parking, not surprising on the relatively small campus, located as it was within the very pricey real estate of North Baltimore and surrounded by exclusive neighborhoods, like Guilford and Homeland. Parking needed a creative solution as soon as possible because it festered and caused frequent temper-laced flare-ups.

Keys were another running sore. Keys to classroom buildings, laboratories, student housing, and laundries were in a chaotic state, when they could be located, and were constantly being borrowed by campus employees and not returned or misplaced and added to the phantom inventory of keys that were permanently out there. Traffic flow on the most congested roadways and driveways snarled movement on the best of days or nights; add a nasty weather scene and "slow movement" became "stop." So vehicular traffic was slow on the best days; add a campus-wide event, and disorder threatened. Property went missing on a regular basis, permanently so, even from rooms supposed to be secured, a disheartening development at a Catholic college. The training of employees had been left to chance, too often the end result of incremental decision making he had seen so often before.

Security employees consisted of inexperienced youths in their first job, serving beside a few grizzled veteran retired cops, together with former corrections officers. Such an employee pool fulfilled the diverse security functions side by side, often with diametrically opposed outlooks on the functions and rationale for the security service.

Steve Tabeling took the time to walk the breadth of the charming campus and visit as many people as he could, asking about their concerns, fears, and disappointments with the security service. He observed the conditions of the roads, the living halls, and the lecture halls, always absorbing information that might prove useful in the future. He found that most of the people were happy with the environment in which they worked, but many could recount an unpleasant incident at some time in the past. A stickler for safety in all its permutations, Tabeling even inspected fire extinguishers— their placement, availability, and condition. He questioned his own people as well about unsafe conditions they had encountered, asking what they had done about them. Most saw immediately that the new director meant business, and that translated to "you better know your job."

But that was the problem: What exactly *was* the job? And what did it entail? At Johns Hopkins, Tabeling had seen that the sense of urgency about being safe was inherently accepted by most people commuting through a high-crime area of the city. No one needed to tell them it was important to be secure. To an extent, the Loyola campus was a bit different.

For starters, most of the daytime students were barely out of their teens and had been raised by devoted parents in a safe and affluent environment. Like most young people, they were often quite trusting, even of strangers. Trust, of course, is a good thing, except when it's misplaced. Just so, those very same parents were, understandably, very protective of their children, and woe to the security employee cornered by an angry parent just discovering unlocked doors in a dormitory building or, worse, strangers lurking therein. The issue would be minutely examined by the chain of authority, rectifications and apologies made, and then, just as probably, forgotten. Until the next dust-up.

The essential problem with security is that while everybody wants to be safe, few are willing to endure the minute inconveniences that being safe entails.

So during his walking and talking tours of the campus, Tabeling amassed reams of data, information the he needed to do his job. And as his analytical mind sorted deficiencies, he saw "things to do right now" and "things to do as soon as the money can be gotten."

The college president fully backed his new security director. Loyola was a successful enterprise, but money could not just be wished from the air. Tabling understood this as well as anyone. He proceeded systematically.

But first a distraction: thefts of items from supposedly locked buildings. Tabeling again adapted prosaic items to house hidden cameras. In no time, a maintenance man was caught in the act, summoned to Steve's office, shown the incriminating video, and fired. Part of his prolific thievery was possible because he was a black hole of keys. Keys came into his possession but never left there. He had unlimited access at any hour and used that to steal. One thief less. But that hardly addressed the issue.

It was the system itself that was the problem. Thousands of keys were floating and who-knew-where or in whose possession, which negated the concept of locked doors. When anybody had the ability to acquire the means of unauthorized access, there was no security.

He began to study alternate systems to conventional locking mechanisms and found a card-reader system that looked promising. With each card assigned to one person permanently, loss or theft became less an issue. If one was lost or stolen, it would immediately be known because the purpose of the system was not just to permit entry but also to record the date and time, the door, and the person who used it in each instance. Thus, a history of card use was created and the data stored, should it be necessary to examine it in the future. Misuse of the card was known instantly and could result in disciplinary action. The system was a tight one.

As Tabeling floated trial balloons, there was resistance, which he had anticipated. Warm discussions ensued. On the one hand, it would entail extensive reconstruction; necessitate unanticipated expense; and be a nuisance. Plus, the data had to be tracked by computer, logging the innumerable daily and hourly premises entries, and collect and collate them by date, building, user, and so on. Worse than all of these, it smacked of Big-Brotherism, similar to parental oversight, a disheartening proposition to young people who had just managed to flee the nest. The campus complaints were innumerable, but over time, and quietly, Tabeling was able to get money to pay for the new security project and convince enough decision makers that card readers were the way to go. Once they were reality, compliance ensued, and soon, incidents of thefts fell to virtually nothing. Significantly, moms and dads loved the concept of the cards and were vociferous in their praise of the new arrangement.

That issue resolved, Tabeling turned his attention to definitive post assignments because he fully understood that an area with security members assigned to no particular area provided inadequate or zero coverage. Taking skills he'd developed at Salisbury, he applied workload formulas to the campus but adapted them to more adequately reflect campus needs. Constant coverage was a basic need. Each new post included its specific protocol, with one member assigned to each building each shift. Those members were strictly tasked to gain full understanding of the structure with the physical layout, including emergency exits, fire extinguisher stations, number of residents and their identities, and similar knowledge. Optimum patrol times were calculated and used as a standard of performance. Report writing was standardized and instituted, and training was provided to ensure proficiency.

Though not intended to be a police department, Steve knew that many of the best features of the law enforcement world were very good fits on a college campus. That accomplished, he turned his attention to the enforcement powers of his members. When the position was offered, he understood that the enforcement members held the status of security officers but without arrest powers, which struck him as totally inadequate. The absence of arrest powers relegated the employees to "catch and hold for the police," about the same capabilities of store security guards.

Modern problems involved a wide range of capabilities—it was not unheard of for serious offenses to take place on or adjacent to the campus. He approached the Maryland State Police and requested their assistance in the acquisition of special police powers. The selection process was highly rigorous and involved fingerprinting of the employees and full background checks, but all the employees qualified, and the security force received a significant upgrade.

Tabeling's security surveys of the property were still ongoing. He noticed that large portions of the campus were inadequately lighted, and he embarked on a comprehensive program to upgrade the illumination and make the brightness consistent throughout. The governing board of directors agreed with the effort and supported it financially.

Parking, that bane of most security directors, constantly caused issues that took much time to sort out. Tabeling noticed that rather than the students poaching parking spots on the faculty lots, the opposite was happening. Many of the faculty, tenured luminaries, felt quite put out when reminded they were expected to use faculty lots. Some protested, but Steve was able, through use of his gifts of persuasion and diplomacy, to help them gain insight into such behavior on the part of highly respected educators. Over time, the problems abated. Not to say that the students were exempt from immature behavior when caught parking in an unauthorized manner and ticketed. As often occurred, privilege, family, and connections were invoked to make the matter go away. Tabeling finally hit a solution—he obtained the services of Howard Gersh, a distinguished member of the Maryland bar and former long-term state's attorney attached to the Homicide Unit. Using his extensive jurisprudence expertise, he presided over a campus traffic "court" that adjudicated parking cases in a strict but equitable manner. The existence of a formal hearing process put a damper on students contemplating scofflaw parking patterns in the future, and the problem diminished. On the opposite hand, Tabeling took it upon himself to appear on behalf of Loyola students who found themselves before a court of law on minor charges—underage drinking, for example, getting them released to him and detailed to the campus administration, with court records expunged.

Human resource numbers usually proved inadequate, especially when emergencies or unplanned-for issues happened. Campus concerts exacerbated this. Rather than hiring additional full-time members, Tabeling petitioned Father Sellinger to hire off-duty Baltimore police officers to supplement campus security; he approved it, and the program succeeded capably.

To address campus traffic congestion, he approached the Cathedral of Mary Our Queen, a magnificent house of worship just down Charles Street from the campus and blessed with tons of parking spaces. They agreed to let students park their personal vehicles on their lots, and Steve procured buses to shuttle them to and from the campus on a regular basis. Congestion problem solved.

During these years at Loyola, he completed an advanced degree in school management and organization, a complete reversal of his once-implacable distaste for anything educational. By then he held two master's degrees and two advanced degrees. Along with his penchant for leadership, he had discovered a love of learning and teaching.

Steve Tabeling found himself utterly content. He still located the occasional fire that needed extinguishing, but most workdays coalesced into inspections and review, verbal reporting from his supervisors, and briefings of his superiors. He had become not unlike an orchestra leader. After much rehearsal and practice, the campus had become his symphony.

Steve III playing with the orchestra at the 50th Wedding
Anniversary Party given by their children.

Steve and Honey 1980

EPILOGUE

S teve Tabeling's retirement from Loyola did not spell the end of his working days. On the contrary, he was still a commodity on the employment market. Frank Napfel, a former sergeant with the Baltimore Police Department, swooped first and instantly hired Steve as a private investigator for Frank's very successful security company, where Tabeling's unique and assorted set of skills could be employed to advantage. The work was challenging and varied, and it kept his interest keen and his skills fine-tuned. After two years, he was approached by a representative from the Baltimore Police Department who recruited him to do some heavy-duty training—a fifty-two-week commitment to conduct classes for the annual state-mandated in-service training, during which every one of the twenty-six hundred Baltimore police officers attended, in addition to numerous officers from outside agencies. The topics included searches and, of course, seizures; stops on the street; reasonable suspicion and how it must be documented; and related subjects. After that year, the police commissioner asked him to return to the agency on a semi-permanent contractual basis and lend his considerable knowledge to the members. He began a nine-year stint at the academy, instructing thousands of new recruits and veteran officers on similar law-related issues, most of which were quite topical and remain so in modern policing.

He found time during these demanding schedules to collaborate on the creation and production of seminars for law enforcement officers around the state and in northern Virginia, where officers and deputies attended his classes. The Homicide Investigator's School was well attended whenever presented and included as instructors current and former homicide investigators, state's attorneys, laboratory technicians, and the deputy state medical examiner, among others, in a demanding weeklong program simulating the discovery, investigation, arrest, and subsequent testimony in a simulated courtroom environment. A more generic five-day seminar imparted similar skills and perspectives for general-purpose investigators. Other successful privately produced law enforcement seminars followed and were highly regarded.

During this time it increasingly came to his attention that some dissatisfaction among command members of the Baltimore Police Department existed; a complaint centered on the relatively low homicide clearances achieved, together with the fact that state's attorneys were hesitant to try some of the cases when suspects had been arrested. Tabeling was asked to perform an exhaustive and in-depth look at the Baltimore Police Department's Homicide Unit.

The study that resulted cited numerous serious issues, not merely with the unit but with the larger organization as well. Though the nature of violence on Baltimore's streets had changed into a more frequently seen stranger-to-stranger murder, most undoubtedly induced by illicit narcotics trade and more difficult to solve, Tabeling's critique and criticisms regarding the Homicide Unit included the premature loss, through reassignment or retirement, of highly productive detectives and their replacement by members not quite ready to take the reins. Other factors played a significant role. He found inadequate or nonexistent sharing of intelligence information between and among critical units of the department; a frequently observed lack of interview skills; and inadequate courtroom testimony acuity. He recommended more intensive and topic-related skills training and a need for mentoring. He noted logistical shortfalls as to computer availability and a perceived antipathy between the detectives and some members of the State's Attorney's Office. The report confirmed what many in the police department had felt to be the case, but it stressed that no quick fix was forthcoming. Only steady and consistent improvements, made a day at a time, would repair what was broken.

When he could, Tabeling was interviewed by local media as violence in the city spiked. He continued his classes at the academy and developed a moot court with the cooperation of University of Baltimore law professor Robert Anderson, during which recruits—working on a simulated case, formulated and investigated in the classroom at Tabeling's direction—prepared to testify. A Circuit Court judge sat as acting judge as the recruits filed into the simulated court room at the university. Third-year law students also observed under the guidance of actual state's attorneys. Actual defense attorneys mentored and conducted the defense in each case. It was a living learning experience and well received by both groups of students, who recognized that doing something was the very best way to learn it. Steve's courtroom innovations produced a more confident student, able to approach the witness stand, bolstered by worthwhile training that improved performance.

But then one day in December 2005, all of the achievements of his life came to nothing when his cherished lifelong friend and wife, suffering more than a year with severe breathing problems, succumbed. Steve's life veered at that moment back to the world and all its cruelty. They lay together in those last hours, surrounded by their adult children and grandchildren. They spoke of baking cookies, family dinners past, and Christmases of long years before. Throughout the night, in whispers, tears, and laughter, they spoke of family and of the love they had for each other and how rich their lives together had been and still was. Before morning's first light, she was gone.

Steve carried on and now works to share his knowledge and experience, only with much younger students. Diving into the deep end yet again, he became a substitute teacher in a large and complex county education system. He fields weekly assignments from first grade through high school, teaching reading, math, and even music; giving back. The terrors of his childhood are now a faint memory, replaced with optimism about today and tomorrow. And good feelings about people.

Turns out the boy who hated school was a born teacher.

POSTSCRIPT

T he tall teacher wore a dark suit and tie, not at all like other teachers. As he stood quietly before the second-grade class, one little boy noticed the tiny gold badge affixed to his lapel.

"Hey, mister, you a police officer?" he asked.

"Not anymore," Steve responded. "But I was once. Long ago."

Warming to this imposing man in their midst, first thing in the morning, other questions followed.

Wrinkling her nose, a little girl raised her hand and asked, "How old are you?"

"Would it matter if I told you?" he replied. "Let's just say that I'm old enough to know a few things. Old enough to be your ..." And the children called out the relationship most supposed, and the word *grandfather* was the most frequent word heard.

Steve smiled and said, "Maybe so. But there's a little girl in this class"—his eyes scanned the students—"and her name is Abigail." As he approached her, she popped from her seat and hugged the tall, well-dressed man and giggled.

He was her absolute favorite teacher, she said, her great-grandfather.

"CHILDREN, GRANDCHILDREN AND GREAT GRANDCHILDREN"

"Steve III, Jason, "Little" Honey,
Patti, Sondra, Dottie and Steve IV

Steve's 89th Birthday Celebration
July 16, 2018

"Old Timers" Crab Feast - September 2016